T5-AGR-226

THE GROUNDWORK OF CRITICISM

JUDGING POETRY

THE GROUNDWORK OF CRITICISM

JUDGING POETRY

BY

STANLEY C. GLASSEY

Senior English Master
Bradford Grammar School

GREENWOOD PRESS, PUBLISHERS
WESTPORT, CONNECTICUT

Library of Congress Cataloging in Publication Data

Glassey, Stanley Churchill.
The groundwork of criticism.

Reprint of the 1947 ed. published by Oxford University Press, London.
1. Poetry. I. Title.
PN1031.G55 801'.951 73-7455
ISBN 0-8371-6934-8

Originally published in 1947 by Oxford University Press, London

This reprint has been authorized by the Clarendon Press Oxford

Reprinted in 1974 by Greenwood Press,
a division of Williamhouse-Regency Inc.

Library of Congress Catalog Card Number 73-7455

ISBN 0-8371-6934-8

Printed in the United States of America

CONTENTS

ACKNOWLEDGEMENTS

THANKS are due to the following for permission to reprint copyright poems:

Messrs. Chatto & Windus and the author's executors for the poems 'Futility' and 'Mental Cases' by Wilfred Owen; Mrs. W. B. Yeats and Messrs. Macmillan & Co. Ltd. for the poem 'An Irish Airman Foresees his Death' from the *Collected Poems of W. B. Yeats*; Mrs. Binyon and the Society of Authors for the poems 'The Little Dancers' and 'For the Fallen' by Laurence Binyon; Messrs. The Hogarth Press for the poems 'As One who Wanders into Old Workings' and 'The Flight' by C. Day Lewis; Mrs. G. Freeman and Messrs. Macmillan & Co. Ltd. for the poem 'The Eye' by John Freeman; Messrs. Macmillan & Co. Ltd. and Mr. Ralph Hodgson for his poem 'Eve'; Messrs. Faber & Faber Ltd. for the poems 'Aunt Helen', 'The Waste Land', 'Animula', and 'Preludes III and IV' from *Collected Poems 1909–1935* by T. S. Eliot and 'An Elementary Classroom' and 'The Express' from *The Still Centre and Poems* by Stephen Spender; the Oxford University Press for the poems 'Against Anger' by Anne Ridler, 'The Tarn' by J. Redwood Anderson, and 'Andromeda' by Gerard Manley Hopkins; and the Clarendon Press, Oxford, for the poem 'Cheddar Pinks' from *New Verse* by Robert Bridges.

INTERPRETATION

CHAPTER I

WHAT IS POETRY?

FOR as far back as history records man has tried to tell, in some form or other, of his experiences, not only in the field of endeavour and achievement, but in that of the emotions, love, hate, hope, and despair, triumph and regret, sorrow and joy. These records of human experience have taken many diverse forms, and the various arts, music, painting, sculpture, literature, and the rest, bear witness to that diversity; but, whatever form the record takes, it reveals a desire to pass on to the future the deeds and thoughts of the present. Of course, it is only in relatively few cases that this desire has come to fruition. Much the greater part of art is short-lived. It may fail to attract attention at all. It may attract and hold attention for a brief time. It may persist for a generation or two, and then fade from the minds of men.

Some art, however, for reasons that have never been, and possibly never will be adequately explained, seems to bear within it the power to persist, some mysterious seed of immortality. It would almost seem as though there is a kind of language *within language*, a power of appealing to, and being understood by, men of many generations and of many races. As with art in general, so with literature, and in particular with poetry.

The search for this mysterious power, this inner and secret language, is a search that will not be fully successful, but, though it may not reveal *the* secret, it will open up so many ways of understanding, and so many avenues of enjoyment, that it will prove well worth undertaking for its own sake.

Our inquiry will be then directed, not to find out that

mysterious secret which has eluded the grasp of so many, but to find out those secrets which can to some extent be grasped, and the discovery of which will throw some light, at any rate, on the study of literature.

We shall consider poetry only, because it is in poetry that the supreme literary artists of almost every age and every race have expressed themselves. What is poetry? No answer to this question has ever met with universal approval. The following judgements are to be considered, not as definitions, or even universally accepted criteria, but rather as starting-points for our own inquiries:

1. Nothing can please many, and please long, but just representations of general nature.

   DR. SAMUEL JOHNSON

2. It is important to hold fast to this: that poetry is at bottom a criticism of life; that the greatness of a poet lies in his powerful and beautiful application of ideas to life. MATTHEW ARNOLD

3. The grand power of poetry is its interpretative power... the power of so dealing with things as to awaken in us a wonderfully full, new, and intimate sense of them, and of our relations with them. MATTHEW ARNOLD

4. The end of Poetry is to produce excitement in co-existence with an overbalance of pleasure.

   WILLIAM WORDSWORTH

5. All good poetry is the spontaneous overflow of powerful feelings. WILLIAM WORDSWORTH

6. Poetry is the breath and finer spirit of all knowledge; it is the impassioned expression which is the countenance of all Science. WILLIAM WORDSWORTH

7. A poet in our times is a semi-barbarian in a civilized community. T. L. PEACOCK

8. Poetry was the mental rattle that awakened the attention of intellect in the infancy of civil society.

T. L. PEACOCK

9. Poetry, in a general sense, may be defined to be 'the expression of the imagination': and poetry is connate with the origin of man. P. B. SHELLEY

10. A poem is the very image of life expressed in its eternal truth. P. B. SHELLEY

11. In common things that round us lie
Some random truths he can impart,
The harvest of a quiet eye
That broods and sleeps on his own heart.

WILLIAM WORDSWORTH

12. Poets are the trumpets that sing to battle, they are the unacknowledged legislators of the world.

P. B. SHELLEY

13. Poetry is life seen through a temperament. IGNOTUS

14. Poetry is everything; it can define the indefinable; it can embrace the illimitable; it can speak the ineffable; it can penetrate the abyss; it can measure eternity.

Il verso è tutto . . . può definire l'indefinibile e dire l'ineffabile; può abbraciare l'illimitato e penetrare l'abisso; può avere dimensioni d'eternità.

GABRIELE D'ANNUNZIO

15. Poetry is emotion recollected in tranquillity.

WILLIAM WORDSWORTH

16. Poetry should be brief, passionate, intense.

EDGAR ALLAN POE

17. The poet is a man who has a greater knowledge of human nature and a more comprehensive soul than are supposed to be common among mankind.

WILLIAM WORDSWORTH

18. Sculpte, lime, cisèle;
Que ton rêve flottant
Se scelle
Dans le bloc résistant!

THÉOPHILE GAUTIER

19. Primarily poetry is an exploration of the possibilities of language. It does not aim directly at consolation or moral exhortation; nor at the expression of exquisite moments, but at an extension of significance; and it might be argued that a too self-conscious concern with 'contemporary' problems deflects the poet's efforts from his true objective. MICHAEL ROBERTS

20. I would say that the poet may write about anything provided that that thing matters to him to start with, for then it will bring with it into the poem the intellectual or moral significance which it has for him in life.

LOUIS MACNEICE

21. *A Poet!*—He hath put his heart to school,
Nor dares to move unpropped upon the staff
Which Art hath lodged within his hand—must laugh
By precept only, and shed tears by rule.
Thy Art be Nature; the live current quaff.

WILLIAM WORDSWORTH

22. Poetry means the *best* words in the best order.

S. T. COLERIDGE

23. What is poetry? The suggestion, by the imagination, of noble grounds for the noble emotions.

JOHN RUSKIN

24. No man was ever yet a great poet, without being at the same time a profound philosopher. S. T. COLERIDGE

25. The business of a poet, said Imlac, is to examine, not the individual, but the species; . . . he does not number

> the streaks of the tulip, or describe the different shades in the verdure of the forest. SAMUEL JOHNSON

It would seem from the foregoing quotations that poets and critics, and especially poet-critics, differ considerably among themselves, not merely about what constitutes poetry, but about what sort of person the poet is, and what is, and even should be, his attitude to poetry.

Thus Dr. Johnson dwells upon the representative nature of poetry. Poetry, he considers, should be an accurate reflection of human life and experience, that is, of general experience. Matthew Arnold inclines to the same view, though he emphasizes points that Dr. Johnson ignores. Arnold stresses the potency and beauty of the poet's work, its power to stir us strongly and deeply. T. L. Peacock argues that poetry is an activity of primitive man, and that its survival is merely a continuation of primitive elements into modern life. William Wordsworth claims that poetry at its best is the spontaneous reaction of the poet to the common experiences of life, though elsewhere he implies that there is often a considerable time-lag between the experiences and the 'spontaneous' reaction. To P. B. Shelley a poet would almost seem to be a prophet and a revolutionary, leading the vanguard in man's thrust towards enlightenment and emancipation. A modern poet, Michael Roberts, finds in the emotive use of language the most natural function of the poet, another, Louis Macneice, sees in the poet's sincerity, his preoccupation with those experiences in life which affect him most strongly, his true dynamic. Théophile Gautier, a French Romantic poet, stresses less the matter than the manner of poetry. The poet is to him an artist working with words, fashioning out of the rude and stubborn mass of personal experience a timeless monument.

Later on it may be of interest, and it certainly will be of value, to study how far, and in what way, poets have applied to their own work their own guiding principles, or—what is perhaps more reasonable—to see to what extent their principles may be deduced from their poetry.

Exercises

Examine each of the following poems or passages of poetry in the light of one or more of the foregoing quotations:

1. The world is too much with us; late and soon,
   Getting and spending, we lay waste our powers:
   Little we see in Nature that is ours;
We have given our hearts away, a sordid boon!

This Sea that bares her bosom to the moon,
   The winds that will be howling at all hours
   And are up-gather'd now like sleeping flowers,
For this, for everything, we are out of tune;

It moves us not.—Great God! I'd rather be
   A Pagan suckled in a creed outworn,
So might I, standing on this pleasant lea,
   Have glimpses that would make me less forlorn;
Have sight of Proteus rising from the sea;
   Or hear old Triton blow his wreathéd horn.

WILLIAM WORDSWORTH

2. Peace to all such! but were there one whose fires
True genius kindles, and fair fame inspires;
Blest with each talent and each art to please,
And born to write, converse, and live with ease:
Should such a man, too fond to rule alone,
Bear, like the Turk, no brother near the throne,
View him with scornful, yet with jealous eyes,
And hate for arts that caus'd himself to rise;
Damn with faint praise, assent with civil leer,
And without sneering, teach the rest to sneer;
Willing to wound, and yet afraid to strike,
Just hint a fault, and hesitate dislike;
Alike reserv'd to blame, or to commend,
A timorous foe, and a suspicious friend;
Dreading ev'n fools, by flatterers besieg'd,
And so obliging, that he ne'er obliged;

Like Cato, give his little senate laws,
And sit attentive to his own applause;
While wits and templars ev'ry sentence raise,
And wonder with a foolish face of praise—
Who but must laugh, if such a man there be?
Who would not weep if Atticus were he?

ALEXANDER POPE

3. *Claudio.* Ay, but to die, and go we know not where;
To lie in cold obstruction and to rot;
This sensible warm motion to become
A kneaded clod; and the delighted spirit
To bathe in fiery floods, or to reside
In thrilling regions of thick-ribbed ice;
To be imprison'd in the viewless winds,
And blown with restless violence round about
The pendent world; or to be worse than worst
Of those that lawless and incertain thought
Imagines howling:—'tis too horrible!
The weariest and most loathed worldly life
That age, ache, penury, and imprisonment
Can lay on nature is a paradise
To what we fear of death.

WILLIAM SHAKESPEARE

4. O, wert thou in the cauld blast,
On yonder lea, on yonder lea;
My plaidie to the angry airt,
I'd shelter thee, I'd shelter thee;
Or did misfortune's bitter storms
Around thee blaw, around thee blaw,
Thy bield should be my bosom,
To share it a', to share it a'.

Or were I in the wildest waste,
Sae black and bare, sae black and bare,
The desert were a paradise,
If thou wert there, if thou wert there.
Or were I monarch of the globe,
Wi' thee to reign, wi' thee to reign,
The brightest jewel in my crown,
Wad be my queen, wad be my queen.

ROBERT BURNS

5. I know that I shall meet my fate
Somewhere among the clouds above;
Those that I fight I do not hate,
Those that I guard I do not love;
My country is Kiltartan Cross,
My countrymen Kiltartan's poor,
No likely end could bring them loss
Or leave them happier than before.
Nor law, nor duty bade me fight,
Nor public men, nor cheering crowds,
A lonely impulse of delight
Drove to this tumult in the clouds;
I balanced all, brought all to mind,
The years to come seemed waste of breath,
A waste of breath the years behind
In balance with this life, this death.

W. B. YEATS

6. Not, Celia, that I juster am
Or better than the rest;
For I would change each hour, like them,
Were not my heart at rest.

But I am tied to very thee
By every thought I have;
Thy face I only care to see,
Thy heart I only crave.

All that in woman is adored
In thy dear self I find—
For the whole sex can but afford
The handsome and the kind.

Why then should I seek further store,
And still make love anew?
When change itself can give no more,
'Tis easy to be true.

SIR CHARLES SEDLEY

7. Move him in the sun—
Gently its touch awoke him once,
At home, whispering of fields unsown.
Always it woke him, even in France,

Until this morning and this snow.
If anything might rouse him now
The kind old sun will know.

Think how it wakes the seeds,—
Woke, once, the clays of a cold star.
Are limbs, so dear-achieved, are sides,
Full-nerved—still warm—too hard to stir?
Was it for this the clay grew tall?
—O what made fatuous sunbeams toil
To break earth's sleep at all?

WILFRED OWEN

8. Sunset and evening star,
And one clear call for me!
And may there be no moaning of the bar,
When I put out to sea,

But such a tide as moving seems asleep,
Too full for sound and foam,
When that which drew from out the boundless deep
Turns again home.

Twilight and evening bell,
And after that the dark!
And may there be no sadness of farewell,
When I embark;

For tho' from out our bourne of Time and Place
The flood may bear me far,
I hope to see my Pilot face to face
When I have crost the bar.

LORD TENNYSON

9. A casement high and triple-arch'd there was,
All garlanded with carven imageries,
Of fruits and flowers, and bunches of knot-grass,
And diamonded with panes of quaint device,
Innumerable of stains and splendid dyes,
As are the tiger-moth's deep-damask'd wings;
And in the midst, 'mong thousand heraldries,
And twilight saints, and dim emblazonings,
A shielded scutcheon blush'd with blood of queens and kings.

JOHN KEATS

10. Near yonder copse, where once the garden smiled,
And still where many a garden flower grows wild;
There, where a few torn shrubs the place disclose,
The village preacher's modest mansion rose.
A man he was to all the country dear,
And passing rich with forty pounds a year;
Remote from towns he ran his godly race,
Nor e'er had changed, nor wished to change his place;
Unpractised he to fawn, or seek for power,
By doctrines fashioned to the varying hour;
Far other aims his heart had learned to prize,
More skilled to raise the wretched than to rise.
His house was known to all the vagrant train,
He chid their wanderings, but relieved their pain;
The long remembered beggar was his guest,
Whose beard descending swept his aged breast;
The ruined spendthrift, now no longer proud,
Claimed kindred there, and had his claims allowed,
The broken soldier, kindly bade to stay,
Sat by his fire, and talked the night away;
Wept o'er his wounds, or tales of sorrow done,
Shouldered his crutch, and showed how fields were won.

OLIVER GOLDSMITH

11. Do not expect again a phoenix hour,
The triple-towered sky, the dove complaining,
Sudden the rain of gold and heart's first ease
Tranced under trees by the eldritch light of sundown.

By a blazed trail our joy will be returning:
One burning hour throws light a thousand ways,
And hot blood stays into familiar gestures.
The best years wait, the body's plenitude.

Consider then, my lover, this is the end
Of the lark's ascending, the hawk's unearthly hover:
Spring season is over soon and first heatwave;
Grave-browed with cloud ponders the huge horizon.

Draw up the dew. Swell with pacific violence.
Take shape in silence. Grow as the clouds grew.
Beautiful brood the cornlands, and you are heavy;
Leafy the boughs—they also hide big fruit.

C. DAY LEWIS

12. Not on the vulgar mass
Called 'work', must sentence pass,
Things done, that took the eye and had the price;
O'er which, from level stand,
The low world laid its hand,
Found straightway to its mind, could value in a trice:

But all, the world's coarse thumb
And finger failed to plumb,
So passed in making up the main account;
All instincts immature,
All purposes unsure,
That weighed not as his work, yet swelled the man's amount.

ROBERT BROWNING

13. He there does now enjoy eternall rest
And happy ease, which thou dost want and crave,
And further from it daily wanderest:
What if some little paine the passage have,
That makes fraile flesh to feare the bitter wave?
Is not short paine well borne, that brings long ease,
And layes the soule to sleepe in quiet grave?
Sleepe after toyle, port after stormie seas,
Ease after warre, death after life, does greatly please.

EDMUND SPENSER

14. Behold her, single in the field,
Yon solitary Highland Lass!
Reaping and singing by herself;
Stop here, or gently pass!
Alone she cuts and binds the grain,
And sings a melancholy strain;
O listen! for the vale profound
Is overflowing with the sound.

No nightingale did ever chant
More welcome notes to weary bands
Of travellers in some shady haunt,
Among Arabian sands:
A voice so thrilling ne'er was heard
In spring-time from the cuckoo-bird,
Breaking the silence of the seas
Among the farthest Hebrides.

Will no one tell me what she sings?
  Perhaps the plaintive numbers flow
For old, unhappy, far-off things,
  And battles long ago:
Or is it some more humble lay,
Familiar matter of to-day?
Some natural sorrow, loss, or pain,
That has been, and may be again?

Whate'er the theme, the maiden sang
  As if her song could have no ending;
I saw her singing at her work,
  And o'er the sickle bending;
I listen'd, motionless and still;
And, as I mounted up the hill,
The music in my heart I bore,
Long after it was heard no more.

WILLIAM WORDSWORTH

15. How sweet I roam'd from field to field
And tasted all the summer's pride,
Till I the Prince of Love beheld
Who in the sunny beams did glide!

He show'd me lilies for my hair
And blushing roses for my brow;
He led me through his gardens fair
Where all his golden pleasures grow.

With sweet May dews my wings were wet,
And Phoebus fir'd my vocal rage;
He caught me in his silken net,
And shut me in his golden cage.

He loves to sit and hear me sing,
Then, laughing, sports and plays with me;
Then stretches out my golden wing,
And mocks my loss of liberty.

WILLIAM BLAKE

16. Mysterious Night! when our first parent knew
  Thee, from divine report, and heard thy name,
  Did he not tremble for this lovely frame
This glorious canopy of light and blue?

Yet 'neath a curtain of translucent dew,
  Bathed in the rays of the great setting flame,
  Hesperus with the host of heaven came
And lo! creation widened in man's view.
Who could have thought such darkness lay concealed
  Within thy beams, O sun! or who could find,
  Whilst fly, and leaf, and insect stood revealed,
  That to such countless orbs thou mad'st us blind!
Why do we then shun Death with anxious strife?
If Light can thus deceive, wherefore not life?

BLANCO WHITE

17. Note in your reading other 'definitions' or 'starting-points' for judgements in literature, and apply them to chosen poems or extracts.

CHAPTER II

KINDS OF POETRY

ONE of the hindrances to the real appreciation, and perhaps even to the enjoyment of poetry, has been the man who has confused the function of critic with that of censor, and who, in consequence, has been inclined to limit the field of poetry to the area of his own predilections. Disliking certain types of culture, and having no understanding of certain types of experience, he has promoted his personal tastes to the rank of absolute standards. Such a one will tell us that the poetry of Dryden and Pope is second-rate because it is almost exclusively didactic or satiric, and that the poetry of Herrick is second-rate because it seems to him to lack high purpose. Another will tell us that Milton's *Paradise Lost* is not poetry at all, because to him true poetry, like human love, is 'brief, passionate, intense'. It lives for a moment of rare exaltation, and then ceases to be. A true poem is, in his view, by its very nature short. Another will disdain the poetry of Robert Browning or T. S. Eliot because he finds it unintelligible, or that of Wordsworth because it is simple. But whatever may be the vagaries of human critics, there is a critic whose judgement is infallible. That critic is Time. Of the rest we may say with Sir Thomas Browne: 'The greater part must be content to be as though they had not been, to be found in the register of God, not in the record of man.'

Bearing in mind our fallibility and transience we may address ourselves to the legitimate task of deepening our enjoyment of poetry by attempting to understand it. We may, for example, wonder why the tags and repetitions characteristic of old ballads, which have in no way lost their power to please, become intolerable in a modern poem, and why figurative language is with one poet a mode of apprehension, by which he sees into the very life of things, and with another a mere means of adornment. We may wonder why in one narrative poem descriptive passages clog the action, whereas in another description is everything. We may wonder why a moralizing or sententious element gives life and character to some lyric poems though such an element seems alien to the very spirit of lyricism. We may wonder why prolixity and digression, which kill the interest in some poems, give added charm to others. The mere putting of these and innumerable other questions opens the way to an understanding of poetry, its mystery, and charm; the decisive, authoritative answer locks, bolts, and bars the door to all further approach.

We must learn to regard all judgements, especially our own, merely as tentative and suggestive, giving useful angles from which to view poems and poets, temporary criteria by which to test, not merely what we read, but ourselves, the readers. If we do this we need never be afraid of giving rein to our own enthusiasms, however extravagant, or of listening to criticisms, however extreme.

It will be useful, too, to remember that though all good poetry has a common origin, a passionate interest in human experience, and the desire and power to give expression to that interest, there are different modes of utterance. Some poets, as more or less detached spectators, tell a story of such aspects of human comedy or tragedy as interest them, others sing of their own sorrows and joys, others attack the follies and crimes of human society or of individuals. Some even express in poetry their views on philosophical or religious problems, or try to recapture the spirit of the heroic age in their country's history. But whether the poet writes narrative, lyric, satiric, didactic, or epic poetry, the true standard of criticism will be, not whether he has chosen a higher or lower mode of poetry, a more or less dignified range of subject-matter, but whether in his own way he has made poetry of his subject, whether he has written in such a manner as to delight, not an age or a coterie, but all men for all time. That will be the measure of his achievement.

Then, again, we may bear in mind that different kinds of poems, with apparently different subject-matter, have the same essential element. The difference lies in the method of treatment. Wordsworth's *Michael* and Burns's *To a Mouse* both have as their basic theme the seeming futility of life and labour. In both the essential conclusion appears to be that

> The best-laid schemes o' mice an' men,
> Gang aft agley,
> An' lea'e us nought but grief and pain,
> For promised joy.

In *Michael*, however, we follow the fortunes of an old man and his son in a long and detailed poem. In *To a Mouse* we are shown a short series of sharply defined pictures. In *Michael*, despite the sadness of the conclusion, we are left with the impression that the life of Michael was a glorious failure, redeemed by an old man's courage and devotion. It is in the story of the old man's struggle that the interest of the poem lies. In *To a Mouse* the reader appears to derive no satisfaction from the frustrations of life, except aesthetic pleasure, the supreme delight of hearing a thing well said.

Futility is the dominant note, too, in Pope's great satire, *The Rape of the Lock.* But here it is a futility which moves us not to tears but to laughter. The poem is narrative in form. It tells a story. It presents human characters and shows them in action. But the main purpose appears to be not to tell a story but to kill folly by ridicule.

Futility, the futility of life and human institutions is a dominant note in much modern poetry, especially that inspired by the Great War of 1914–18.

It may now be of interest to study the differences between the above-mentioned modes of poetry, and try to discover what, if any, are fundamental.

Lyric Poetry

Lyric poetry is, perhaps, the earliest form of poetry. The first infant, in the very moment of birth, was, it would seem, the first lyric poet:

we came crying hither:
Thou know'st, the first time that we smell the air,
We wawl and cry.

The spontaneous expression of acute desires, in rhythmic utterance, is the essence of lyricism. All true lyric poetry has, as its subject-matter, the individual expression of human lacks and loves, bodily and spiritual cravings, and the emotions connected with them. Love of woman, the great void of death, the appeal of external nature, as they are among the commonest interests of man, so they are among the commonest subjects of lyric poetry. It is for this reason that though highly personal in their inspiration the best lyric poems always strike a universal note. It is this universal in the particular that is indeed the most characteristic mark of the classic lyric. Simplicity in stanzaic structure, facility in the arrangement of the rhyme, simplicity and naturalness in language and sentiment, and spontaneity are characteristic notes of lyric poetry. In Robert Burns, the greatest lyrist in English literature, these characteristics are amply illustrated.

There is, of course, a more elaborated form of lyric, in which more complex emotions are expressed, in more complex stanzaic form, in less simple language. Such Odes as Shelley's *To the West Wind* and Keats's *To a Nightingale* belong to this order of lyric poem.

Then there is another kind, the more sophisticated lyric of the Cavalier poet, in which a slightly worldly-wise urbanity tempers the lyric utterance. The simplicity of language and form remain, the spirit is different. The following passages, representing the different types of lyrics, will illustrate the point:

1. Ye flowery banks o' bonnie Doon,
How can ye bloom sae fair!
How can ye chant, ye little birds,
And I sae fu' o' care!

Thou'll break my heart, thou bonnie bird
That sings upon the bough;
Thou minds me o' the happy days
When my fause Luve was true.

Thou'll break my heart, thou bonnie bird
That sings beside thy mate;
For sae I sat, and sae I sang,
And wist na o' my fate.

Aft hae I roved by bonnie Doon
To see the woodbine twine;
And ilka bird sang o' its love,
And sae did I o' mine.

Wi' lightsome heart I pu'd a rose,
  Frae aff its thorny tree;
And my fause luver staw the rose,
  But left the thorn wi' me.

ROBERT BURNS

2. My heart aches, and a drowsy numbness pains
  My sense, as though of hemlock I had drunk,
Or emptied some dull opiate to the drains
  One minute past, and Lethe-wards had sunk:
'Tis not through envy of thy happy lot,
  But being too happy in thine happiness
  That thou, light-wingéd Dryad of the trees,
      In some melodious plot
  Of beechen green, and shadows numberless,
  Singest of summer in full-throated ease.

O for a draught of vintage! that hath been
  Cool'd a long age in the deep-delved earth,
Tasting of Flora and the country green,
  Dance, and Provençal song, and sunburnt mirth!
O for a beaker full of the warm south,
  Full of the true, the blushful Hippocrene,
  With beaded bubbles winking at the brim,
      And purple-stained mouth;
  That I might drink, and leave the world unseen,
  And with thee fade away into the forest dim.

Fade far away, dissolve, and quite forget
  What thou among the leaves hast never known,
The weariness, the fever, and the fret
  Here, where men sit and hear each other groan;
Where palsy shakes a few, sad, last grey hairs,
  Where youth grows pale, and spectre-thin, and dies;

Where but to think is to be full of sorrow
    And leaden-eyed despairs;
Where Beauty cannot keep her lustrous eyes,
Or new Love pine at them beyond to-morrow.

Three stanzas from *Ode to a Nightingale*
by JOHN KEATS

3\. That which her slender waist confined
Shall now my joyful temples bind:
No monarch but would give his crown
His arms might do what this has done.

It was my Heaven's extremest sphere,
The pale which held that lovely deer:
My joy, my grief, my hope, my love
Did all within this circle move.

A narrow compass! and yet there
Dwelt all that's good, and all that's fair:
Give me but what this ribband bound,
Take all the rest the Sun goes round.

E. WALLER: *On a Girdle*

The Song Lyric

Closely akin to the lyric is the song lyric, which varies from the poem that is scarcely to be differentiated from the lyric to the verse form that is hardly to be recognized as poetry at all. Every year brings forth popular songs of this latter order. The true song lyric is usually distinguishable from the lyric poem in that it is expressive more of some general sentiment than of a personal emotion, whereas the lyric is a personal utterance having a universal application. We feel, for example, that though Robert Burns's *Highland Mary* is a poignant expression of Burns's true love for one of his sweethearts, which also happens to express a passion common to men, Ben Jonson's famous song *Drink to me only with thine eyes* expresses merely a common love sentiment. The following stanzas, the first from Burns's *Highland Mary*, the second from Jonson's *Drink to me only with thine eyes*, will show something of this difference.

1. Wi' mony a vow and lock'd embrace
   Our parting was fu' tender;
And pledging aft to meet again,
   We tore ourselves asunder;
But, oh! fell Death's untimely frost,
   That nipt my flower sae early!
Now green's the sod, and cauld's the clay,
   That wraps my Highland Mary!

2. Drink to me only with thine eyes,
   And I will pledge with mine;
Or leave a kiss but in the cup
   And I'll not look for wine.
The thirst that from the soul doth rise
   Doth ask a drink divine;
But might I of Jove's nectar sup,
   I would not change for thine.

Frequently, too, the song lyric is attuned to the atmosphere of some play in which it occurs. Songs in Shakespeare are almost always adapted to the spirit of the play and the idiosyncrasies of some of the characters. For example, in *Twelfth Night*, the song

Come away, come away, death,
   And in sad cypress let me be laid;
Fly away, fly away, breath;
   I am slain by a fair cruel maid.
My shroud of white, stuck all with yew,
      O, prepare it!
My part of death, no one so true
      Did share it.

harmonizes admirably with the sentimentality of Duke Orsino and the Lady Olivia, and is attuned to the opening speech of the Duke,

If music be the food of love, play on;
Give me excess of it, that, surfeiting,
The appetite may sicken, and so die. . . .

In *The Tempest* Ariel's songs 'Come unto these yellow sands' and 'Full fathom five thy father lies' are in keeping, not only with the daintiness of the unbodied sprite Ariel, but with the character of the scene in which they occur.

We should find it interesting and useful to compare songs which have become literature with popular songs which have not, to try to discover what those of the first class possess which is lacking in those of the second class.

Narrative Poetry

Though narrative poetry, as its name implies, is poetry which tells a story, its boundary lines are extremely difficult to draw. Many narrative poems contain elements of epic, philosophical, and satiric poetry. In some the narrative element is of less importance to the reader than the spirit or atmosphere of the poem.

Matthew Arnold's *Sohrab and Rustum* is mainly a narrative poem telling the old story of the duel between the young Sohrab and his father Rustum, in which the father unwittingly kills his son. *Balder Dead*, also by Arnold, tells how the blind god, Hoder, slew the beloved god Balder through the treachery of the perfidious Loki. These are narrative poems, touched here and there by something of the epic spirit. Coleridge's *Ancient Mariner* and *Christabel* gain the reader's interest less by the story as such than by the spirit of incantation, with which the poem is invested. Byron's *Don Juan* is a vast poem in which narrative, lyric, and satiric elements combine to form a poem of great power. Such poems as his *Corsair* and *The Bride of Abydos* are pure romantic narrative poems. Wordsworth's *Michael* would seem to many people a plain unvarnished tale, but there is a bleak heroic grandeur about the old man's life which imparts to the poem not a little of epic dignity. Keats's *Eve of St. Agnes* is a narrative poem, a story of medieval romance which tells how a young knight entered the castle of his fierce hereditary foes to carry off his beloved. Here again, the interest of the reader lies at least as much in the atmosphere of long ago, the rich pageantry of the medieval setting, and the charm of frosty moonlight, as in the story itself. Spenser's *Faerie Queene* is an extended allegory, which is virtually a series of narrative poems embodying romantic stories of knightly deeds, invested, as has been said, with an 'atmosphere of moonlight, silvery faint, and pure', in a verse form admirably contrived to charm the ear with its slow and languorous music. Chaucer's *Canterbury Tales* is a collection of narrative poems in which the stories themselves are often of supreme interest, but usually the style in which they are told, admirably adapted to the personality of the supposed narrator, lends powerful aid to the stories themselves.

Satire

Two quotations from Dryden will illustrate the two main purposes of satire, to brand and castigate human viciousness, and to laugh at human folly. Of the first he says:

> ''Tis an action of virtue to make examples of vicious men. They may and ought to be upbraided with their crimes and follies; both for their own amendment, if they are not yet incorrigible, and for the terror of others, to hinder them from falling into those enormities which they see are so severely punished in the persons of others.'

Of the second he says: 'Neither is it true, that this fineness of raillery is offensive. A witty man is tickled while he is hurt in this manner, and a fool feels it not.'

The satire of the Roman poet Juvenal belongs to the first category. Dryden himself affords examples, notably the character of Zimri in *Absalom and Achitophel*, of the second. Much satire does not fall easily into either of these classes. Pope's *Dunciad*, for example, is as severe as if it were being applied to the castigation of real viciousness in others, instead of to the satisfaction of Pope's own spitefulness. So, too, with his description of Lord Hervel (Sporus) in the *Epistle to Dr. Arbuthnot*. Famous satires in English literature are Pope's *Dunciad* and *Rape of the Lock*, Dryden's *Absalom and Achitophel*, and Byron's *Vision of Judgement*.

The following satiric portraits, though by no means fully representative of English satire, will give some idea of its range:

1. Some of their chiefs were princes of the land:
In the first rank of these did Zimri stand:
A man so various, that he seemed to be
Not one, but all mankind's epitome.
Stiff in opinions, always in the wrong,
Was everything by starts, and nothing long;
But in the course of one revolving moon
Was chymist, fiddler, statesman, and buffoon;
Then all for women, painting, rhyming, drinking,
Besides ten thousand freaks that died in thinking.
Blest madman, who could every hour employ
With something new to wish, or to enjoy!
Railing and praising were his usual themes,
And both, to show his judgement, in extremes:
So over violent, or over civil,
That every man with him was God or Devil.

In squandering wealth was his peculiar art;
Nothing went unrewarded but desert.
Beggared by fools, whom still he found too late,
He had his jest, and they had his estate.

JOHN DRYDEN.

2. Yet let me flap this bug with gilded wings,
This painted child of dirt, that stinks and stings;
Whose buzz the witty and the fair annoys,
Yet wit ne'er tastes, and beauty ne'er enjoys:
So well-bred spaniels civilly delight
In mumbling of the game they dare not bite.
Eternal smiles his emptiness betray,
As shallow streams run dimpling all the way.
Whether in florid impotence he speaks,
And, as the prompter breathes, the puppet squeaks;
Or at the ear of Eve, familiar toad,
Half froth, half venom, spits himself abroad,
In puns, or politics, or tales, or lies,
Or spite, or smut, or rhymes, or blasphemies.
His wit all see-saw, between that and this,
Now high, now low, now master up, now miss,
And he himself one vile antithesis.
Amphibious thing! that acting either part,
The trifling head, or the corrupted heart,
Fop at the toilet, flatterer at the board,
Now trips a lady, and now struts a lord.

ALEXANDER POPE

3. Miss Helen Slingsby was my maiden aunt,
And lived in a small house near a fashionable square
Cared for by servants to the number of four.
Now when she died there was silence in heaven
And silence at her end of the street.

The shutters were drawn and the undertaker wiped his feet—
He was aware that this sort of thing had occurred before.
The dogs were handsomely provided for,
But shortly afterwards the parrot died too.
The Dresden clock continued ticking on the mantel-piece,
And the footman sat upon the dining-table
Holding the second housemaid on his knees—
Who had always been so careful while her mistress lived.

T. S. ELIOT

Elegiac Poetry

Elegiac poetry, as its name implies, is inspired by the poet's sorrow at the death of some loved one. It would therefore seem to belong to the category of lyric poetry. Much elegiac poetry is akin to lyric, both in tone and feeling and in its structure, notably Robert Burns's elegies for Mary Morison and Highland Mary. But there is a kind of English elegy which is too elaborate in structure, and too reflective in treatment to be regarded as purely lyrical. This kind of elegy requires special consideration. It is often traditional, modelled on the elegies of a Greek poet, Theocritus, who flourished in Sicily in the third century B.C., transmitted through Italian influence to French literature, and thence to English literature. Spenser's collection of poems, *The Shepherd's Calendar*, contains several examples of the kind.

Because of the period in which Theocritus wrote, the setting of the old Greek elegy was naturally pastoral, and the poems themselves dealt with the incidents of a shepherd's life. The setting and much of the description of the rustic life itself became traditional in elegiac poetry. As Professor Herford says:

'Certain traditional forms Theocritus fixed upon the pastoral for all time; the singing match for some rustic wager, a soft white lamb, a carven drinking bowl of beech-wood or of maple; the bout of rude bantering between two rival swains; the sad lament of a lover for unrequited or deceived love; the dirge of his fellows around the tomb of some dead shepherd, Daphnis or another, who in his time had himself well known to build the lofty rhyme among them.'

English pastoral elegy followed the traditional form, not only in the pastoral setting, in the reference to the shepherds' lives and loves, to their singing contests and rivalry, but even in the pastoral turn, a convention whereby the mood of sadness is tempered by a strain of consolation. Milton in his *Lycidas*, a lament not so much for Edward King in particular as for ideal spiritual beauty and nobility, preserved some of the traditions of the form. Shelley in his *Adonais*, an elegy on the death of John Keats, has some traces of the pastoral tradition.

Not all the longer and reflective English elegiac poems embody the pastoral convention. For example, the most famous of all, *Gray's Elegy in a Country Churchyard*, which reflects on the general subject of death rather than on the loss of a loved one, is completely lacking in the conventions of the pastoral. So, too, is Cowper's *Lines on the Receipt of my Mother's Picture*.

Of the following passages, the first, from Milton's *Lycidas*, illustrates not only the pastoral tradition in general, but the conventional pastoral elegiac 'turn' in particular. The second from Shelley's *Adonais* illustrates the pastoral elegiac 'turn'.

1. Weep no more, woeful shepherds, weep no more,
For Lycidas, your sorrow, is not dead,
Sunk though he be beneath the watery floor;
So sinks the day-star in the ocean-bed,
And yet anon repairs his drooping head
And tricks his beams, and with new-spangled ore

Flames in the forehead of the morning sky:
So Lycidas sunk low, but mounted high
Through the dear might of Him that walk'd the waves;
Where, other groves and other streams along,
With nectar pure his oozy locks he laves,
And hears the unexpressive nuptial song
In the blest kingdoms meek of joy and love.
There entertain him all the saints above
In solemn troops, and sweet societies,
That sing, and singing in their glory move,
And wipe the tears for ever from his eyes.
Now, Lycidas, the shepherds weep no more;
Henceforth thou art the Genius of the shore
In thy large recompense, and shalt be good
To all that wander in that perilous flood.

2. Peace, peace! he is not dead, he doth not sleep—
He hath awakened from the dream of life—
'Tis we, who lost in stormy visions, keep
With phantoms an unprofitable strife,
And in mad trance, strike with our spirit's knife
Invulnerable nothings.—*We* decay
Like corpses in a charnel; fear and grief
Convulse us and consume us day by day,
And cold hopes swarm like worms within our living clay.

He has outsoared the shadow of our night;
Envy and calumny and hate and pain,
And that unrest which men miscall delight,
Can touch him not and torture not again;
From the contagion of the world's slow stain
He is secure, and now can never mourn
A heart grown cold, a head grown gray in vain;
Nor, when the spirit's self has ceased to burn,
With sparkless ashes load an unlamented urn.

He lives, he wakes—'tis Death is dead, not he;
Mourn not for Adonais.—Thou young Dawn,
Turn all thy dew to splendour for from thee
The spirit thou lamentest is not gone;
Ye caverns and ye forests, cease to moan!
Cease ye faint flowers and fountains, and thou Air,
Which like a mourning veil thy scarf hadst thrown
O'er the abandoned Earth, now leave it bare
Even to the joyous stars which smile on its despair!

He is made one with Nature: there is heard
His voice in all her music, from the moan
Of thunder, to the song of night's sweet bird;
He is a presence to be felt and known
In darkness and in light, from herb and stone,
Spreading itself where'er that Power may move
Which has withdrawn his being to its own;
Which wields the world with never-wearied love,
Sustains it from beneath, and kindles it above.

He is a portion of the loveliness
Which once he made more lovely: he doth bear
His part, while the one Spirit's plastic stress
Sweeps through the dull dense world, compelling there,
All new successions to the forms they wear;
Torturing th'unwilling dross that checks its flight
To its own likeness, as each mass may bear;
And bursting in its beauty and its might
From trees and beasts and men into the Heaven's light.

Epic Poetry

Epic poetry reflects the spirit of the heroic age in a nation's history, and usually retails the exploits of the great heroes of primitive times. Homer's *Iliad*, for example, tells the story of the siege of Troy, and glorifies the deeds of the Greek and Trojan heroes who fought round its walls. The great French epic, the *Chanson de Roland*, records the heroic deeds of Roland, the famous warrior of Charlemagne's army, and his glorious stand with his comrades Oliver and Archbishop Turpin at Roncesvaux. *Beowulf*, the Old English epic poem, celebrates the struggle of the warrior Beowulf against the dragons Grendel and Grendel's dam, who had ravaged Heorot. Besides these are great poems, such as Virgil's *Aeneid*, which reflect something of the epic feeling, but are affected by the tone of a literary age, and lack something of the vitality, spontaneity, simplicity, and freshness of true epic, though they lack nothing of its patriotic feeling.

Philosophic and Didactic Poetry

The eighteenth century, a great age for satiric poetry, was also notable for a type of poetry which flourished strongly in no other age of English literature, namely, philosophical and didactic poetry, poetry intended to instruct by amusing, or to amuse by instructing. Dryden's *Religio Laici*, Pope's *Essay on Man*, and his *Essay on Criticism* are the most noteworthy examples of this kind. The merits of this poetry are cogency of argument, aptness of illustrative detail, and epigrammatic brilliance of diction. The following passages taken respectively from the *Essay on Criticism* and the *Essay on Man* will illustrate the virtues and perhaps the weaknesses of this kind of poetry.

1. Others for language all their care express,
And value books, as women men, for dress:
Their praise is still,—the style is excellent:
The sense, they humbly take upon content.
Words are like leaves; and where they most abound,
Much fruit of sense beneath is rarely found:

False eloquence, like the prismatic glass,
Its gaudy colours spreads on every place;
The face of nature we no more survey,
All glares alike, without distinction gay:
But true expression, like the unchanging sun,
Clears and improves whate'er it shines upon,
It gilds all objects, but it alters none.
Expression is the dress of thought, and still
Appears more decent, as more suitable;
A vile conceit in pompous words expressed,
Is like a clown in regal purple dressed:
For different styles with diff'rent subjects sort,
As sev'ral garbs with country, town, and court.

ALEXANDER POPE

2. Look next on greatness; say where greatness lies?
'Where, but among the heroes and the wise?'
Heroes are much the same, the point's agreed,
From Macedonia's madman to the Swede;
The whole strange purpose of their lives, to find
Or make, an enemy of all mankind?
Not one looks forward farther than his nose.
No less alike the politic and wise;
All sly slow things, with circumspective eyes:
Men in their loose unguarded hours they take,
Not that themselves are wise, but others weak.
But grant that those can conquer, these can cheat;
'Tis phrase absurd to call a villain great:
Who wickedly is wise, or madly brave,
Is but the more a fool, the more a knave.
Who noble ends by noble means obtains,
Or failing, smiles in exiles or in chains,
Like good Aurelius let him reign or bleed
Like Socrates, that man is great indeed.

ALEXANDER POPE

CHAPTER III

INFLUENCES

It is an axiom of social science that however strongly individualistic a particular personality may be, however unique his contribution to life, he is inevitably influenced by groups of factors known under the general name of environment. Environment and heredity are considered the two great forces shaping individual destiny.

But environment is a very general term indeed. It includes many things. It includes, for example, geographical environment, it includes general social environment, it includes particular social environment. A man's work may be influenced by the fact that he is born in, or early in life removes to, a busy industrial or commercial centre, or that he is born in and never emerges from some secluded valley. It may be influenced by the fact that his immediate family environment is cultured or uncultured, politically conscious or otherwise, ardently revolutionary, or socially and politically reactionary. It may be influenced by the wider social environment. It may be influenced by the fact that he is living in some age relatively cut off from or exposed to cultural influences from abroad. Shakespeare, for example, lived in an age when for Englishmen all the horizons, geographical, intellectual, and spiritual, were opening out as if to infinity. He came to London at a comparatively early age, and at a time when he would be in contact with all those who were helping to shape the new social, political, and intellectual tendencies of a robust age of expansion. He would be in contact with the sea captains and explorers of the New World, with the University wits and scholars who were making available, not only the intellectual wealth of the ancient world, but the literature of Italy, Spain, and France, and with the politico-religious citizens and divines who were making London a city of religious and political Puritanism. Shakespeare's work does not merely reveal the inventive power of a great original genius, but it reflects also the acquired cultural resources and experience of the scholars, thinkers, and men of action of his day.

Consider, for example, the play *Hamlet*. First of all there is the story itself, obtained from literary sources available in Shakespeare's day, then probably an earlier version of the play, serving as a rough model, and then, worked into the very fabric of the play, a host of contemporary allusions. All this is acquired material, the result of Shakespeare's habit of 'invading authors like a monarch', as one of his contemporaries says. But what is peculiarly Shakespeare's is first the supreme dramatic architecture, the shaping of all this material into a great play, second, the superb poetry of the blank verse dialogue and soliloquies, and third, and perhaps greatest of all, the creation of characters which, though they may stand as types of human beings, are as individual and living as the men and women we see around us, which our ancestors saw, and which doubtless our descendants will see in their turn, Hamlet, King Claudius, his queen Gertrude, Polonius, Laertes, Ophelia, Horatio, Guildenstern and Rosencrantz, or Rosencrantz and Guildenstern, the grave-diggers, and Yorick the jester, more unforgettably alive in his grave than many a man who walks amongst us 'in his habit as he lived'. Had not Shakespeare been born when he was, and come to London when he did, his drama could surely not have been so wide in range, so deep in penetration, and so vital.

His sonnets, too, reveal this fusion of the creative and borrowed elements. The sonnet itself as a literary form was derived from Italian sources, by one of Shakespeare's immediate predecessors. The contemporary English sonnet, like Shakespeare's own, was full of conventionalities common to European sonnet cycles, the dedication to a real or supposed lover, the adjuration to the lover to marry, lest his or her unique charms should not be continued to posterity, the proud claim of immortality for the sonnets, the description of the mistress's charms in terms of the flower garden.

Who will believe my verse in time to come,
If it were fill'd with your most high deserts?
Though yet, heaven knows, it is but as a tomb
Which hides your life and shows not half your parts.
If I could write the beauty of your eyes
And in fresh numbers number all your graces,
The age to come would say 'This poet lies;
Such heavenly touches ne'er touch'd earthly faces.'
So should my papers, yellowed with their age,
Be scorn'd, like old men of less truth than tongue,
And your true rights be term'd a poet's rage
And stretched metre of an antique song:
 But were some child of yours alive that time,
 You should live twice, in it and in my rhyme.

The forward violet thus did I chide:
Sweet thief, whence didst thou steal thy sweet that smells,
If not from my love's breath? The purple pride
Which on thy soft cheek for complexion dwells
In my love's veins thou hast too grossly dyed.
The lily I condemned for thy hand,
And buds of marjoram had stol'n thy hair;
The roses fearfully on thorns did stand,
One blushing shame, another white despair;
A third, nor red nor white, had stol'n of both,
And to his robbery had annexed thy breath;
But, for his theft, in pride of all his growth
A vengeful canker eat him up to death.
 More flowers I noted, yet I none could see
 But sweet or colour it had stol'n from thee.

But, besides these conventionalities, there is revealed in the sonnet an experience of life, expressed with such intensity of bitterness and passion that it can hardly be other than a reflection of Shakespeare's own.

The expense of spirit in a waste of shame
Is lust in action; and till action, lust
Is perjured, murderous, bloody, full of blame,
Savage, extreme, rude, cruel, not to trust;
Enjoy'd no sooner but despised straight;
Past reason hunted; and no sooner had,
Past reason hated, as a swallowed bait,
On purpose laid to make the taker mad:
Mad in pursuit, and in possession so;
Had, having, and in quest to have, extreme;
A bliss in proof, and proved, a very woe;
Before, a joy proposed; behind, a dream.
All this the world well knows; yet none knows well
To shun the heaven that leads men to this hell.

Something of this same bitter sense of the evil in life, an acute suffering, whether personal or vicarious, is reflected, not only in the great tragedies, but also in that little group of comedies which are akin to tragedies, *Much Ado About Nothing*, *Measure For Measure*, and *All's Well That Ends Well.*

This fusion of personal and second-hand experience, under the stimulus of a creative energy unique in English literature for its penetration and intensity, is not the least interesting aspect of the study of Shakespeare.

But Shakespeare is, as we have seen, partly a unique creative artist, and partly the product of his age, one of the characteristics of which was the fresh vigour of its artistic creation. This freshness and vigour, this zest for life and new experience, this sense of the glory and beauty of life are apparent throughout Elizabethan literature, as well in the outburst of lyric poetry which marked the age as in the drama of Shakespeare's contemporaries and immediate predecessors. Sometimes these elements are found yoked to strange spiritual fellows. Thus the poetry of Edmund Spenser, which is marked by all the Elizabethan love of beauty, the sense of the glory and freshness of life strongly affected by the spirit of the Italian Renaissance, is also deeply tinged with that Puritanism which in some of its manifestations was afraid of and hostile to beauty. An awareness of the presence of both elements is vital to a full understanding of the poetry of Spenser. The following two stanzas from the second book of the *Faerie Queene*, which occur in one of the most sensuously beautiful passages in English literature, the description of the Bower of Acrasia and its lovely 'damzelles', represent, but by no means adequately, the two opposing influences.

So passeth, in the passing of a day,
Of mortall life the leafe, the bud, the flowre,
No more doth flourish after first decay,
That earst was sought to decke both bed and bowre
Of many a Ladie, and many a paramowre:
Gather therefore the Rose, whilest yet is prime,
For soone comes age, that will her pride deflowre:
Gather the Rose of love, whilest yet is time,
Whilest loving thou mayst loved be with equall crime.

But all those pleasaunt bowres, and Pallace brave,
Guyon broke downe, with rigour pittilesse;
Ne ought their goodly workmanship might save
Them from the tempest of his wrathfulnesse;
But that their blisse he turn'd to balefulnesse:
Their groves he feld, their gardins did deface,
Their arbers spoyld, their Cabinets suppresse,
Their banket houses burne, their buildings race,
And of the fairest late, now made the fowlest place.

It is impossible to do more than indicate the usefulness of possessing some knowledge of the influences moulding a writer. Some further instances readily suggest themselves.

Cowper was in one vital respect the antithesis of Shakespeare. While Shakespeare loved and sought a wide experience of life, Cowper shunned all but a narrow circle of his fellow creatures. This circle included the ladies of the Unwin household, whose influence was all to his good, and the Rev. Mr. Newton, an over-zealous Evangelical curate, who encouraged in Cowper a mood of spiritual pessimism which was partly congenital. Cowper's poetry reflects this limitation as clearly as it reflects the positive elements in Cowper's personality, his acquired calm and serenity and his fits of morbid despair. The following passages will illustrate the two influences at work upon Cowper.

Now stir the fire, and close the shutters fast,
Let fall the curtains, wheel the sofa round,
And while the bubbling and loud-hissing urn
Throws up a steamy column, and the cups,
That cheer but not inebriate, wait on each,
So let us welcome peaceful evening in.
Not such his evening, who with shining face
Sweats in the crowded theatre, and squeez'd
And bored with elbow-points through both his sides
Out-scolds the ranting actor on the stage;
Nor his, who patient stands till his feet throb
And his head thumps, to feed upon the breath
Of patriots bursting with heroic rage,
Or placemen, all tranquillity and smiles.

'Tis pleasant through the loop-holes of retreat
To peep at such a world; to see the stir
Of the great Babel and not feel the crowd;
To hear the roar she sends through all her gates

At a safe distance, where the dying sound
Falls a soft murmur on th'uninjured ear.
Thus sitting and surveying thus at ease
The globe and its concerns, I seem advanced
To some secure and more than mortal height,
That lib'rates and exempts me from them all.
It turns submitted to my view, turns round
With all its generations; I behold
The tumult and am still. The sound of war
Has lost its terrors ere it reaches me;
Grieves, but alarms me not. I mourn the pride
And av'rice that makes man a wolf to man;
Hear the faint echo of those brazen throats
By which he speaks the language of his heart,
And sigh, but never tremble at the sound.

I was a stricken deer that left the herd
Long since; with many an arrow deep infixt
My panting side was charged, when I withdrew
To seek a tranquil death in distant shades.
There was I found by one who had himself
Been hurt by th'archers. In his side he bore,
And in his hands and feet, the cruel scars.
With gentle force soliciting the darts
He drew them forth, and heal'd and bade me live.
Since then, with few associates, in remote
And silent woods I wander, far from those
My former partners of the peopled scene,
With few associates, and not wishing more
Here much I ruminate, as much I may.

Obscurest night involved the sky,
The Atlantic billows roared,
When such a destined wretch as I,
Washed headlong from on board,

Of friends, of hope, of all bereft,
His floating home for ever left.

Not long beneath the whelming brine,
  Expert to swim, he lay;
Nor soon he felt his strength decline,
  Or courage die away;
But waged with death a lasting strife,
Supported by despair of life.

He long survives, who lives an hour
  In ocean, self-upheld:
And so long he, with unspent power,
  His destiny repelled:
And ever as the minutes flew,
Entreated help, or cried—'Adieu!'

At length, his transient respite past,
  His comrades, who before
Had heard his voice in every blast,
  Could catch the sound no more:
For then, by toil subdued, he drank
The stifling wave, and then he sank.

No voice divine the storm allayed,
  No light propitious shone,
When snatched from all effectual aid,
  We perished, each alone:
But I, beneath a rougher sea,
And whelmed in deeper gulfs than he.

The following passage illustrates another influence on Cowper's mind, that of the widespread humanitarian spirit which was beginning to awaken in his time.

My ear is pain'd,
My soul is sick with ev'ry day's report
Of wrong and outrage with which earth is fill'd.
There is no flesh in man's obdurate heart,
It does not feel for man. The nat'ral bond
Of brotherhood is sever'd as the flax,
That falls asunder at the touch of fire.

Slaves cannot breathe in England; if their lungs
Receive our air, that moment they are free,
They touch our country and their shackles fall.
That's noble, and bespeaks a nation proud
And jealous of the blessing.

The poetry of the eighteenth century was influenced in many ways. First may clearly be seen a reaction against the 'enthusiasm' which characterized the religious life of many of the Puritans. The unrestrained spiritual outpourings in which zealous Puritans had indulged became synonymous, among the generations which succeeded them, with canting hypocrisy. Hence their suspicion of violent self-revelation of all kinds. It was the mark of a gentleman to keep himself well in hand, to refrain from any undue display of personal feelings. This was doubtless one of many reasons for the drying up of genuine lyrism during this period. When the poet did wish to express his feelings he frequently chose some type of poetry which gave him the opportunity of giving to his own thought the appearance of a common judgement. This partly accounts for Pope's preference for the *Satire*. Here under the cloak of performing a public duty he could veil his contempt for contemporary scribblers and poetasters, statesmen like Lord Hervey, and rivals like Joseph Addison. This desire to express what cultured people in general rather than the poet alone felt is seen, not only in the choice of religious and philosophic subjects, but in the poet's attitude to them.

Hence the versified generalities in such poems as Dryden's *Religio Laici*, and *Hind and the Panther*, Pope's *Essay on Man*, Mark Akenside's *Pleasures of the Imagination*, Gray's exquisite *Elegy in a Country Churchyard*, and Collins's *Odes*.

In the following short extracts, though they are very different in actual choice of subject, the influence of the spirit of the age will be clearly apparent.

Daughter of Jove, relentless power,
  Thou tamer of the human breast,
Whose iron scourge and torturing hour
  The bad affright, afflict the best!
Bound in thy adamantine chain,
The proud are taught to taste of pain,
And purple tyrants vainly groan
With pangs unfelt before, unpitied and alone.

When first thy sire to send on earth
  Virtue, his darling child, designed,
To thee he gave the heavenly birth,
  And bade to form her infant mind.
Stern rugged nurse! thy rigid lore
With patience many a year she bore:
What sorrow was, thou bad'st her know,
And from her own she learned to melt at other's woe.

Wisdom in sable garb arrayed,
  Immersed in rapturous thought profound,
And Melancholy, silent maid,
  With leaden eye that loves the ground,
Still on thy solemn steps attend:
Warm charity, the general friend,
With Justice, to herself severe,
And Pity, dropping soft the sadly-pleasing tear.

From *Hymn to Adversity*, by THOMAS GRAY

Dim as the borrowed beams of moon and stars
To lonely, weary, wandering travellers
Is reason to the soul: and as on high
Those rolling fires discover but the sky,
Not light us here, so Reason's glimmering ray
Was lent, not to assure our doubtful way,
But guide us upward to a better day.
And as those nightly tapers disappear
When day's bright lord ascends our hemisphere,
So pale grows Reason at Religion's sight,
So dies, and so dissolves in supernatural light.
Some few, whose lamp shone brighter, have been led
From cause to cause to Nature's secret head,
And found that one first principle must be;
But what, or who, that UNIVERSAL HE;
Whether some soul encompassing this ball,
Unmade, unmoved, yet making, moving all,
Or various atoms' interfering dance
Leapt into form (the noble work of chance,)
Or this great All was from eternity,
Not even the Stagirite himself could see,
And Epicurus guessed as well as he.
As blindly groped they for a future state,
As rashly judged of Providence and Fate.

From *Religio Laici*, by JOHN DRYDEN

Look next on greatness: say where greatness lies,
Where, but among the heroes and the wise?
Heroes are much the same, the point's agreed,
From Macedonia's madman to the Swede;
The whole strange purpose of their lives to find,
Or make, an enemy of all mankind!
Not one looks backward, onward still he goes,
Yet ne'er looks forward further than his nose.

No less alike the politic and wise;
All sly slow things, with circumspective eyes:
Men in their loose unguarded hours they take,
Not that themselves are wise, but others weak.
But grant that those can conquer, these can cheat;
'Tis phrase absurd to call a villain great:
Who wickedly is wise, or madly brave,
Is but the more a fool, the more a knave.
Who noble ends by noble means obtains,
Or failing, smiles in exile or in chains,
Like good Aurelius let him reign, or bleed
Like Socrates, that man is great indeed.

From the *Essay on Man*, by ALEXANDER POPE

N.B. In this passage is discernible, not merely the spirit of an age, but the experience of all ages.

In Robert Burns, also an eighteenth-century poet, two violently contrasted tendencies may be seen, a strong reaction against his narrow religious environment, the world of 'Holy Willie' and his like, and the equally vigorous expression of his own twin passions for strong drink and fair women. Whether the influence of the religious atmosphere of his age, seen in its better aspects in *The Cottar's Saturday Night*, or his own passions produced the better poetry will be a matter of opinion. There can, however, hardly be much doubt that from these two sources of inspiration flowed a strong and vigorous poetry. Another influence which had a marked effect on Burns's poems and songs was that of the ideas of social and political reform which were to find expression in France in the French Revolution and in England in the social and political progress of the nineteenth century. The following extracts are by no means representative of these influences, and not at all of Burns's more individual inspiration, but they will do something to show that he was affected by his day and generation.

The cheerfu' supper done, wi' serious face,
They, round the ingle, form a circle wide;
The sire turns o'er, wi' patriarchal grace,
The big ha'-Bible, ance his father's pride:
His bonnet reverently is laid aside,
His lyart haffets[1] wearing thin and bare;
Those strains that once did sweet in Zion glide,
He wales[2] a portion with judicious care;
And 'let us worship God!' he says, with solemn air.

The priest-like father reads the sacred page,
How Abram was the friend of God on high;
Or Moses bade eternal warfare wage
With Amalek's ungracious progeny;
Or how the royal Bard did groaning lie
Beneath the stroke of Heaven's avenging ire;
Or Job's pathetic plaint, and wailing cry;
Or rapt Isaiah's wild, seraphic fire;
Or other holy seers that tune the sacred lyre.

Perhaps the Christian volume is the theme,
How guiltless blood for guilty man was shed;
How He, who bore in Heaven the second name,
Had not on earth whereon to lay His head:
How His first followers and servants sped;
The precepts sage they wrote to many a land:
How he, who lone in Patmos banished,
Saw in the sun a mighty angel stand;
And heard great Babylon's doom pronounced by Heaven's
command.

From *The Cottar's Saturday Night*, by ROBERT BURNS

[1] grey side-locks [2] chooses

The lads an' lasses, blythely bent
  To mind baith saul an' body,
Sit round the table, weel content,
  An' steer[1] about the toddy.
On this ane's dress, an' that ane's leuk,
  They're making observations;
While some are cozie i' the neuk,[2]
  An' formin assignations
    To meet some day.

But now the Lord's ain trumpet touts,[3]
  Till a' the hills are rairin,
An' echoes back return the shouts;
  Black Russel[4] is na spairin:
His piercing words, like Highlan swords,
  Divide the joints an' marrow;
His talk o' Hell, where devils dwell,
  Our vera 'sauls does harrow'
    Wi' fright that day.

A vast, unbottom'd, boundless pit,
  Fill'd fu' o'lowin[5] brunstane,
Wha's raging flame, an' scorching heat,
  Wad melt the hardest whun-stane![6]
The half asleep start up wi' fear,
  An' think they hear it roarin,
When presently it does appear,
  'Twas but some neibor snorin
    Asleep that day.

From *The Holy Fair* by ROBERT BURNS

Is there, for honest poverty,
  That hangs his head, and a' that?
The coward-slave, we pass him by,
  We dare be poor for a' that!

[1] stir [2] nook [3] blows [4] Minister of Kilmarnock [5] flaming [6] whinstone

For a' that, and a' that,
Our toils obscure, and a' that;
The rank is but the guinea stamp;
The man's the gowd for a' that.

A prince can mak a belted knight,
A marquis, duke, and a' that;
But an honest man 's aboon his might,
Gude faith, he mauna fa'[1] that!
For a' that, and a' that,
Their dignities and a' that,
The pith o' sense, and pride o' worth,
Are higher rank than a' that.

Then let us pray that come it may,
As come it will for a' that;
That sense and worth, o'er a' the earth,
May bear the gree,[2] and a' that;
For a' that, and a' that,
It 's coming yet, for a' that;
That man to man, the world o'er,
Shall brothers be for a' that.

From *A Man's a Man For A' That*, by ROBERT BURNS

In our time the influence of contemporary events and social movements is seen in the poetry of the 'Great War' of 1914–18 and the next twenty years. The disillusionment which followed hard upon the first years of the war, the slaughter of the great offensives, the miseries of trench warfare, the hard-faced vulgarity of the profiteering classes, the neglect of the fighting men, the breaking of the promises held out in the years of struggle, the complete frustration of the nobler hopes engendered by the war, found expression in a body of poetry which, though very varied both in subject-

[1] manage [2] pre-eminence

matter and treatment, revealed, at any rate among many of the better-known writers, a bitter and ironic pessimism sometimes starkly expressed, and sometimes veiled in an obscurity more telling than direct treatment could possibly be. If we read Laurence Binyon's *For the Fallen* and Rupert Brooke's *The Soldier*, and then Siegfried Sassoon's *They* or *Memorial Tablet*, Isaac Rosenberg's *Dead Man's Dump*, and Wilfrid Owen's *Mental Cases* we shall realize how powerfully after the 'first fine careless rapture' of the war the pressure of events moulded contemporary poetry. It is, of course, true that in a sense all poetry is subjective, the product of a personal impression: the poet can but look out upon life through his own eyes. But between him and the object upon which he gazes is a miasma of blood, sweat, and tears which distorts that which to others seems so fair into a nightmare of horror and repulsion. These aspects of the varied scene on which the modern poet has gazed may be seen with varying degrees of obscurity in such poems as T. S. Eliot's *Difficulties of a Statesman*, a succession of confused images, sometimes related, and sometimes unrelated, suggesting compositely the complete futility of modern statesmanship, *The Hollow Men*, a powerful expression of the pessimism following the Great War of 1914–18, a poem as remarkable for the fineness of individual lines and passages as for the hard brilliance of its sustained gloom; and the more ambitious *The Waste Land*, Stephen Spender's *After They Have Tired*, in which the poet's disgust with the present does not dim his faith in a future where those who follow after may

> Watch the admiring dawn explode like a shell
> Around us, dazing us with light like snow.

An Elementary School Classroom; The Uncreating Chaos; C. Day Lewis's *You That Love England*, with its enigmatic references to the new power in a new world, and *The Conflict!*; and in Ronald Bottrall's *The Future Is Not For Us*, a poem which seems to express disgust with the present and hopelessness for the future.

Yet, interesting as much of this poetry is, we cannot but echo the pious thought with which Stephen Spender concludes *The Uncreating Chaos*,

Holy is lucidity
And the mind that dare explain.

Lucidity is not lacking in some modern poetry which seeks new inspiration in giving poetic life to the commonplace things and experiences of modern life. John Masefield's *Widow in the Bye Street* and many other of his narrative poems; D. H. Lawrence's *Baby Tortoise*, *End of Another Home Holiday*, and *Snake*; J. R. Anderson's *The Bridge*; Siegfried Sassoon's *Morning Express*; Edmund Blunden's *Mole Catcher*; Martin Armstrong's *Miss Thompson Goes Shopping*; and Roy Campbell's *Choosing a Mast* call for little of the ingenious guess-work of the commentator.

It would be impossible in so short a space to show adequately in how many ways modern writers have tried to shape a new poetry out of the new-old material of the life of to-day. All that has been attempted is to show how the poet in shaping the stuff of his poetry has himself been shaped by things and events. If the reader turns to the work of poets mentioned in this short section, and to countless others, this point will be made abundantly clear.

CHAPTER IV

WORDS

Polonius. What do you read, my lord?
Hamlet. Words, words, words.

It will often be necessary to remind ourselves, in our study of poetry, that, whatever a writer's idiosyncrasy may be—

whether like Wordsworth he affects simplicity, or like Keats strives to enrich his poetry with romantic and colourful diction, or like Pope aims at incisiveness, conciseness, and sharpness of contrast, or like some modern poets attempts to capture the reader's imagination with violent or obscure images—whatever, in short, his aim or method may be, the poet's medium is words, and, for the most part, words with which his readers will be familiar.

If we read one of the most difficult of modern poems, Mr. T. S. Eliot's *The Waste Land*, we shall find that with the exception of some foreign words the vocabulary is quite intelligible to a normal person. It is in the use of the words that the difficulty lies. What, for example, are we to make of the following lines?

What are the roots that clutch, what branches grow
Out of this stony rubbish? Son of man,
You cannot say, or guess, for you know only
A heap of broken images, where the sun beats,
And the dead tree gives no shelter, the cricket no relief,
And the dry stone no sound of water. Only
There is shadow under this red rock,
(Come in under the shadow of this red rock),
And I will show you something different from either
Your shadow at morning striding behind you
Or your shadow at evening rising to meet you;
I will show you fear in a handful of dust.

There is not a single word in the passage that a third-form boy would not recognize, and out of the 108 words it contains, 79 are common monosyllabic words, 23 are of two syllables, and 3 only of three syllables.

It is obvious that a first reading conveys little sense to the average person. Only after careful study, a patient examination of the *words* in themselves, and in their combinations, does any sense emerge. We then begin to discover a preponderance of images suggesting death, frustration, or sterility—*stony rubbish*, *broken images*, *dead tree*, *no shelter*. The passage begins to have some meaning for us, though as yet only a vague meaning, in association with the preceding and following passages and with the spirit and content of the whole poem.

Now let us consider, by way of contrast, a stanza from a poem that would have some difficulty for a third-form boy, not because of the obscure way in which quite common words are used, but because of the unfamiliarity of some of the words, words that would present no difficulty to the average adult reader of poetry.

> Far from the madding crowd's ignoble strife,
> Their sober wishes never learned to stray;
> Along the cool sequester'd vale of life
> They kept the noiseless tenour of their way.

The poet Gray is here describing the life of the nameless unambitious villagers, some of whom, though possibly possessed of great but undeveloped talents, preferred living and dying in obscurity to struggling for power and fame.

Here again, though Gray's style is so completely different from T. S. Eliot's, we find the same tendency to let the weight of the meaning rest on some specially significant words, *madding*, *crowd*, *ignoble*, *strife* in the first line being *contrasted* with *sober*, *cool*, *sequestered*, *noiseless* in the following three.

In both these passages the poet seems to be appealing to some emotion which he feels and we share. In the first place he appeals to that emotion of frustration and disgust that we experience when we feel ourselves to be out of harmony with our environment, in the second to that longing for calm serenity which assails us in all the clamour and fury of life, and to our envy of those happy souls who have attained the blessings of ordered tranquillity.

Sometimes the language used by a poet appeals not so much to what are usually called the emotions, fear, happiness, remembered pleasure, the 'thoughts that do often lie too deep for tears', as to an intellectual sense, our sense of the appropriateness and exactness of the poet's perceptions. Such differences may sometimes be hard to define precisely, but they can be felt. In reading the poetry of Burns, for example, we feel in ourselves, especially if we are Scots, something of the poet's own emotion. We live through his experience more or less intensely. We share it. Few can read

But, Mousie, thou art no thy lane
In proving foresight may be vain:
The best laid schemes o' mice and men
  Gang aft a-gley,
An' lea'e us nought but grief an' pain,
  For promised joy.

without for a moment being the poet.

When, however, we read the couplet from Dryden's poem *MacFlecknoe*,

The rest to some faint meaning make pretence,
But Shadwell never *deviates* into sense

the effect of the word 'deviates', its expression of Dryden's contempt for the poetaster Shadwell, and of the latter's pitiful inadequacy is more objective. We rejoice in and admire the poet's verbal play rather than experience the emotions he feels. The difference is perhaps mainly one of degree, yet it is also one of point of view. We are seeing life rather as an interested spectator than as a participant. So, too, with Pope's use of language. We may feel a keen interest as looker-on at the little coterie of ladies he describes with such insight in *The Rape of the Lock*, admire the deftness of his little character touches, but we do not join the party.

In various talk th' instructive hours they past,
Who gave the ball, or paid the visit last;
One speaks the glory of the British Queen,
And one describes a charming Indian screen;
A third interprets motions, looks, and eyes;
At ev'ry word a reputation dies.

We note with satisfaction the deepening tone of the satiric description, as shown by the key-words, *glory*, *charming*, words descriptive of the gushing ladies, *interprets* which suggests the growing seriousness and concentration of the ladies' activity, a *reputation dies* showing how deadly the game is becoming, and how deeply the poison is being injected.

When he is describing the young lady Belinda we are drawn a little more deeply in,

On her white breast a sparkling cross she wore,
Which Jews might kiss, and infidels adore.

But the feeling is only momentary, and we are soon surveying the scene as spectators, not as principals. The emotional tension aroused by the images in the couplet is allayed in the next few lines, and we are again mere lookers-on, not potential victims.

Her lively looks a sprightly mind disclose,
Quick as her eyes, and as unfix'd as those:
Favours to none, to all she smiles extends;
Oft she rejects, but never once offends.

'Lively looks' and 'sprightly mind' suggest once more the purely social scene and occasion.

As spectators, too, we survey the scene portrayed in much narrative and descriptive poetry, where scenes and events are, as it were, catalogued for our inspection. In reading, for example, Coleridge's *This Lime Tree Bower my Prison*, when we come to the passage

The roaring dell, o'erwooded, narrow, deep,
And only speckled by the mid-day sun;
Where its slim trunk the ash from rock to rock
Flings arching like a bridge;—that branchless ash,
Unsunned and damp, whose few poor yellow leaves
Ne'er tremble in the gale, yet tremble still,
Fanned by the water-fall!

we stand as if before a familiar picture, recognizing and enjoying the truth of the artist's conception, and feeling perhaps a flush of renewed pleasure at this and similar scenes. Both creative and re-creative are the words *speckled*, *slim trunk*, *flings arching*, *branchless ash*, *unsunned and damp*. They give its peculiar character to the scene portrayed.

In *Frost at Midnight* we are drawn nearer to the centre of things. We lose ourselves momentarily in the scene. Some of us may even become at one with the poet, as if it were our experience he is describing, as we sit before the fire on a wintry evening

the thin blue flame
Lies on my low-burnt fire, and quivers not;
Only that film, which fluttered on the grate,
Still flutters there, the sole unquiet thing.
Methinks its motion in this hush of nature
Gives it dim sympathies with me who live,
Making it a companionable form,
Whose puny flaps and freaks the idling Spirit
By its own moods interprets.

But, on reading the greatest of Coleridge's poems, *The Ancient Mariner*, we are more than spectators, we more than join the social or family circle, we more than share the hearth. We become the Ancient Mariner himself; we are sole survivor of a doomed crew, living again, and living with frightful intensity those mysterious experiences as

All in a hot and copper sky,
The bloody sun, at noon,
Right up above the mast did stand,
No bigger than the moon.

The words *copper* sky, and *bloody* sun do not describe something that has existed for others. They create something which exists for us, a real world of terror, a nightmare world in which we live isolated by our own guilty fears.

Alone, alone, all, all alone,
Alone on a wide wide sea!
And never a saint took pity on
My soul, in agony.

But it is to Shakespeare we have to turn if we wish to study with what royal power and dignity a supreme poet uses the full resources of language. Whatever the occasion, whatever the mood of the speaker, the language of the poet seems the necessary and inevitable vehicle of expression. It has that mysterious secret of vitality, the power possessed by the very greatest artists, and by them alone, of giving life and character to pen-and-ink and brush-and-colour abstractions. Consider for a moment the passage in *King John* in which Queen Constance mourns over her son Arthur. Every image the poet evokes enables the reader and spectator to see the boy as a mother would see him, in the attitudes and occasions dear to a mother's heart, and though the passage is one long figure of speech, in which 'Grief', an abstract idea, is made to personate the living child, the natural images and homely diction by which they are expressed present him to us, a living reality, 'in his habit as he lived'.

Grief fills the room up of my absent child,
Lies in his bed, walks up and down with me,
Puts on his pretty looks, repeats his words,

Remembers me of all his gracious parts,
Stuffs out his vacant garments with his form;
Then have I reason to be fond of grief.

It is impossible to select particularly significant words or phrases: the whole passage is a succession of vital images.

Now consider the passage in *Coriolanus* in which the envious Brutus describes to his fellow tribune Sicinius the popular reception given to the victorious Roman general Coriolanus.

All tongues speak of him, and the *bleared* sights
Are *spectacled* to see him: your *prattling* nurse
Into a rapture lets her baby cry
While she *chats* him: the kitchen malkin pins
Her *richest lockram* 'bout her *reechy* neck,
Clambering the walls to eye him: *stalls*, *bulks*, *windows*,
Are *smother'd* up, *leads fill'd* and *ridges horsed*
With variable complexions, all agreeing
In earnestness to see him:

The italicized expressions do, to some extent, illustrate the happy use of particular words and concrete images, but it is in the combination of the appropriate selection of elements in the crowd and the words to reveal them naturally that Shakespeare's genius is seen. The word *prattling*, for example, describes the nursemaid, who, whether she is discussing the latest popular hero or scandal, or the latest air raid or world calamity, displays always the same irresponsibility, but it is the association of 'prattling' with the following concrete images of the neglected charge that *fixes* the passage unforgettably.

your *prattling nurse*
Into a rapture *lets her baby cry*
While she *chats* him.

The enumeration of definite parts of buildings, 'stalls', 'bulks', 'windows', 'leads', 'ridges', gives sharpness of outline to the concrete reality of the scene, and the three verbs 'smothered', 'filled', and 'horsed' further strengthen the picture.

Similarly precise, though differing in quality, is the macabre realism of Juliet's speech to Friar Laurence in *Romeo and Juliet*,

> Or shut me nightly in a charnel-house,
> O'er-cover'd quite with dead men's *rattling* bones,
> With *reedy* shanks and *yellow chapless* skulls.

The words 'rattling', 'reedy', 'yellow', and 'chapless' are italicized merely for the purpose of illustration. They are, of course, not italicized in the original.

But it is not only in accuracy of representation that Shakespeare's mastery of words shows itself. It is in the unerring insight with which he uses words, not merely to express the varied emotions of his characters, but to sound deeply the answering emotion in the hearts of his readers, or of spectators at the theatre. Of such a quality is the passage in which Prospero expresses not only his own poignant sense of the enigma of human existence, and the phantasmal nature of experience, but a feeling which has ever haunted the human mind.

> These our actors,
> As I foretold you, were all spirits, and
> Are melted into air, into *thin air:*
> And, like the *baseless fabric* of this *vision*,
> The cloud-capped towers, the gorgeous palaces,
> The solemn temples, the great globe itself,
> Yea, all which it inherit, shall *dissolve*,
> And, like this *insubstantial pageant faded*,
> Leave not a rack behind. We are such *stuff*
> As *dreams* are made on; and our *little* life
> Is rounded with a *sleep*.

The words and phrases *thin air*, *baseless fabric*, *vision*, *dissolve*, *insubstantial pageant*, *stuff*, *dreams*, *little*, *sleep* are, of course, of peculiar significance in this passage.

There is another aspect of Shakespeare's use of language which compels notice, his use of metaphor. Shakespeare does not *use* figurative language in the sense that other writers appear to use it. He seems to think in metaphor, to see things in relation to other things, and in terms of other things. His figurative language ranges from the pure conceit to the most penetrating analysis of life. In his early plays his metaphors are often merely fanciful, not, be it noted, so much conscious adornments of thought, as the ebullitions of a lively mind playing a little below the surface of things, apprehending skin-deep similarities. In his later plays it becomes the instrument of a powerful imagination reaching deep down into the secret places of the heart.

Compare, for example, Romeo's speech at the monument, charged with emotion though it may be, with Macbeth's speech on learning of the death of his wife, or that to his wife when he is plotting the murder of Banquo.

O my love! my wife!
Death, that hath suck'd the honey of thy breath,
Hath had no power yet upon thy beauty:
Thou art not conquer'd; beauty's ensign yet
Is crimson in thy lips and in thy cheeks,
And death's pale flag is not advanced there.

. . . . .

Ah, dear Juliet,
Why art thou yet so fair? shall I believe
That unsubstantial death is amorous,
And that the lean abhorred monster keeps
Thee here in dark to be his paramour?

For fear of that, I still will stay with thee,
And never from this palace of dim night
Depart again: here, here will I remain
With worms that are thy chamber-maids; O, here
Will I set up my everlasting rest,
And shake the yoke of inauspicious stars
From this world-wearied flesh.

[*as he swallows poison*]

Come, bitter conduct, come, unsavoury guide!
Thou desperate pilot, now at once run on
The dashing rocks thy sea-sick weary bark.
Here 's to my love.

In this speech, despite its emotional unity, and the general quality, there are degrees of metaphorical penetration. Some of the earlier images are either conventional or at the level of the conventional, *the honey of thy breath*, *beauty's ensign*, *death's pale flag*. The figures of the middle passage, such as *lean abhorred monster*, *his paramour*, are of Shakespearian boldness and vigour, and though to *some* tastes they may appear a little strained they are consistent with the emotional quality of the passage and help to intensify it. The macabre allusion in the passage

here will I remain
With worms that are thy chamber-maids

may strike *some* as straining the general conception of the middle passage almost to jarring point. The images in the last few lines are distinctly at the conventional level, and perceptibly lower the emotional tone.

The figurative language of the two passages from *Macbeth* has all the elements of Shakespearian metaphor at its greatest. It lays bare the pitiful tragedy of Macbeth's frustrated life, its insensate strugglings and bitter nullity.

She should have died hereafter;
There would have been a time for such a word.
To-morrow, and to-morrow, and to-morrow,
Creeps in this petty pace from day to day,
To the last syllable of recorded time;
And all our yesterdays have lighted fools
The way to dusty death. Out, out brief candle!
Life's but a walking shadow, a poor player
That struts and frets his hour upon the stage
And then is heard no more: it is a tale
Told by an idiot, full of sound and fury,
Signifying nothing.

Lady M. What's to be done?
Macb. Be innocent of the knowledge, dearest chuck,
Till thou applaud the deed. Come seeling night,
Scarf up the tender eye of pitiful day,
And with thy bloody and invisible hand
Cancel and tear to pieces that great bond
Which keeps me pale! Light thickens, and the crow
Makes wing to the rooky wood.

In the first passage there is a procession of images suggesting the emptiness of human existence, *creeps in*, *petty pace*, *fools*, *brief candle*, *walking shadow*, *poor player*, *struts and frets*, *a tale told by an idiot*, *signifying nothing*. In the second the metaphor of the blinding of the hawk, followed by that of the cancellation of Banquo's lease of life, 'that great bond that keeps me pale', is surpassed in imaginative intensity by the memorable picture of the fall of night, expressing symbolically the closing in of the shadows of evil upon Macbeth,

Light thickens, and the crow
Makes wing to the rooky wood.

In both these passages, despite the fact that the metaphors are frequently on different planes of thought, there is complete emotional harmony in the expression. The impression left on the mind is single and memorable.

There is the same artistic consistency in the figurative language which so often forms the stuff of his expression in the blank verse of his earlier plays, but here the language is usually fanciful rather than deeply and penetratively imaginative. Witness, for example, that passage in *Romeo and Juliet* in which Romeo speaks of Juliet as she appears at a window:

But, soft! what light through yonder window breaks?
It is the east, and Juliet is the sun!
Arise, fair sun, and kill the envious moon,
Who is already sick and pale with grief,
That thou her maid art far more fair than she:
Be not her maid, since she is envious;
Her vestal livery is but sick and green,
And none but fools do wear it; cast it off.
It is my lady; O, it is my love!
O, that she knew she were!
She speaks, yet she says nothing: what of that?
Her eye discourses, I will answer it.
I am too bold, 'tis not to me she speaks:
Two of the fairest stars in all the heaven,
Having some business, do intreat her eyes
To twinkle in their spheres till they return.

and that in *The Merchant of Venice* spoken by Bassanio after he has opened the leaden casket and discovered the picture of Portia.

Fair Portia's counterfeit! What demi-god
Hath come so near creation? Move those eyes?
Or whether, riding on the balls of mine,
Seem they in motion? Here are sever'd lips,
Parted with sugar breath: so sweet a bar
Should sunder such sweet friends. Here in her hairs

The painter plays the spider, and hath woven
A golden mesh to entrap the hearts of men,
Faster than gnats in cobwebs: but her eyes,—
How could he see to do them? having made one,
Methinks it should have power to steal both his
And leave itself unfurnish'd.

The images in the first passage, the comparison of the window at which Juliet appears to the east, and Juliet herself to the sun, the succeeding comparison of her eyes to stars are not, strictly speaking, conceits but rather conventional metaphors strained to hyperbole. In the second, though there is a similar tendency to hyperbolic metaphor, that of *the painter playing the spider* is a pure conceit. In both passages the imagery is attuned to the emotional character of the scene.

So far we have considered Shakespeare's language in fairly long passages, and the range of illustration has been correspondingly limited. The pregnancy of Shakespeare's language in general, and metaphor in particular, can be just as well seen in short passages, with scarcely any reference to their contexts. Consider, for example, a line and a half already quoted:

Light *thickens*, and the crow
Makes wing to the *rooky* wood.

All the phenomena of oncoming night are vividly impressed upon our imaginations by the italicized words. The peculiar dusk of evenfall cannot be better expressed than by the word *thickens*, or the heavy laboured flight of the crow than by the phrase *makes wing*, which inevitably draws our eyes to the slow flapping of its wings, while the adjective *rooky* applied to wood suggests the darkening shade in the tree-tops, and both, phrase and adjective, reinforce the impression of gathering dusk, and more penetratingly still the gradual darkening of the soul of a great man by the suffusing power of evil.

What speech could give more adequate definition to a character than the line and a half in which Enobarbus portrays the timeless charm of Cleopatra?

Age cannot *wither* her, nor custom *stale*
Her *infinite variety*.

All Othello's tragedy is impressed in his brief apostrophe of Desdemona:

O thou *weed*,
Who art so *lovely fair* and *smell'st so sweet*
That the *sense aches* at thee.

the italicized words and phrases show clearly enough what terrible reinforcement sensual passion gave to his jealousy.

Popular philosophy and experience find, in *Hamlet*, a complete if brief expression in the King's remark to his wife,

When sorrows come, they come not *single spies*,
But in *battalions!*

Again in *Hamlet* the commonest of all human experiences finds pointed expression in the King's vivid metaphor,

There lives within the very *flame of love*
A kind of *wick* or *snuff* that will *abate* it.

In the same play Laertes and his father Polonius express indirectly the same thought

For Hamlet, and the *trifling* of his favour,
Hold it a *fashion*, and a *toy in blood*,
A *violet* in the youth of *primy nature*.

I do know,
When the *blood burns*, how *prodigal* the soul
Lends the *tongue vows*.

As the italicized words and phrases show, in all three of these short passages love is represented, in varied metaphor, as a transient upthrust of young physical nature.

In *Macbeth*, the agonized remorse of a murderer, almost unhinged by his frenzied imagination, is unforgettably fixed by Macbeth's words

> No; this my hand will rather
> The *multitudinous seas incarnadine.*

Often in Shakespeare a mere phrase will illumine a dramatic situation, and give full personality to a character. Witness in *Antony and Cleopatra* Charmian's apostrophe of the dying Cleopatra 'O Eastern Star!', or in *Hamlet* Laertes' reference to his sister Ophelia 'O rose of May', or in *Coriolanus* Coriolanus's apostrophe to his wife 'My gracious silence'.

It is almost impossible to *isolate* aspects of the connotation of a word, and dwell exclusively on one or other of them, the purely intellectual aspect of a word, its *meaning*, in the general sense of that word, its musical quality, or its power of evoking a scene or a smell, or stimulating any other sense. Various aspects of sense merge so completely into the unity of the word that isolation is often very difficult. But it is possible to *perceive* such individual aspects. It is possible, too, to note how two different sense aspects of the same word or phrase combine to produce a particular appeal. For example, the familiar phenomenon of the rising moon is admirably presented to us by the opening lines of a sonnet by Sir Philip Sidney,

> With how *sad* steps, O Moon, thou *climb'st* the skies!
> How silently, and with how *wan* a face!

Here the familiar experience is re-created for us partly by the slow majestic rhythm of the lines, partly by the meaning or suggestion of the word *climb'st*, and partly by the visual image evoked by the word *wan.* Again, that other vision of the moon with which we are familiar, the *appearance* of the moon when clouds are driven by the wind between earth and moon, and the moon *seems* to dip to let them pass, is presented sharply to our minds by the lines in Milton's *Il Penseroso*,

> To behold the *wandering* Moon
> *Riding* near her highest noon,
> Like one that had been led *astray*
> Through the heaven's wide *pathless* way,
> And oft, as if her head she *bow'd*
> *Stooping* through a fleecy cloud.

The words *wandering*, *riding*, *astray*, *pathless*, *bow'd*, *stooping*, and the stately movement of the lines, to which these words of course contribute, combine to form a clear picture.

This particular aspect of the connotation of words, the picture-suggestiveness of words, whether or not in conjunction with other sense-aspects, is too obvious, of course, to be missed. Some examples of this have been noted in another connexion, others may with advantage be studied here. In the following passage from Coleridge's *Christabel*, a familiar sight of the dying Autumn, the last dead leaf clinging precariously to the tree-top, is impressed upon our mind by the triple suggestiveness of the words 'red', 'dance', 'hanging so light' and 'topmost twig':

> There is not wind enough to twirl
> The one *red* leaf, the last of its clan,
> That *dances* as often as dance it can,
> *Hanging so light*, and hanging so high,
> On the *topmost twig* that looks up at the sky.

Consider now the opening stanza of Keats's *Ode to Autumn*, and in particular the italicized words *bend*, *moss'd*, *swell*, *plump*, and the underlined word *clammy*.

Season of mists and mellow fruitfulness,
Close bosom-friend of the maturing sun;
Conspiring with him how to load and bless
With fruit the vines that round the thatch-eaves run;
To *bend* with apples the *moss'd* cottage-trees,
And fill all fruit with ripeness to the core;
To *swell* the gourd, and *plump* the hazel shells
With a sweet kernel; to set budding more,
And still more, later flowers for the bees,
Until they think warm days will never cease;
For Summer has o'erbrimm'd their clammy cells.

The three words *bend*, *swell*, and *plump*, especially the last word 'plump', give a peculiarly concrete visual image of the fullness of harvest, while *moss'd* suggests a familiar picture of an orchard. Clammy gives a very precise tactile sense-image.

In the following short passage, spoken by Cleopatra to her attendant Iras, in the play *Antony and Cleopatra*, the concrete visual image conveyed by the words *mechanic*, *greasy*, *rules* and *hammers* can to some extent be isolated, but it is merged in and forms a unity with the emotional intention and effect of the whole passage.

Now, Iras, what think'st thou?
Thou, an Egyptian puppet, shalt be shown
In Rome, as well as I: *mechanic* slaves
With *greasy aprons*, *rules* and *hammers*, shall
Uplift us to the view—in their thick breaths,
Rank of gross diet, shall we be enclouded
And forced to drink their vapour.

Sense and Sound

The musical quality of words, alone or in combination, is also an important element in poetic technique, though too deliberate or apparently over-emphasized onomatopoeic effects may be distasteful. In the last resort personal taste must decide. What to a fastidious ear may appear unbearable may be even pleasing to a taste less nice. The following passage from Tennyson's *Morte D'Arthur*, with its preponderance of harsh consonantal combinations, k-sounds and nasal sounds, obviously suggests *to the ear* as well as to the understanding the figure of a steel-clad knight striding over rocky mountain paths.

> Dry clash'd his harness in the icy caves
> And barren chasms, and all to left and right
> The bare black cliff clang'd round him, as he based
> His feet on juts of slippery crag that rang
> Sharp-smitten with the dint of armèd heels—
> And on a sudden, lo! the level lake,
> And the long glories of the winter moon.

The quiet tone of the last two lines puts into sharp relief the harsh clangour of the first five.

Equally obvious in its onomatopoeic effect, and presumably intention, is the following passage from Matthew Arnold's poem *The Strayed Reveller*,

> They see the Heroes
> Sitting in the dark ship
> On the foamless, long-heaving,
>   Violet sea:
> At sunset nearing
> The Happy Islands.

The rhythm of the third line, and the harmonizing of the dominant vowel sounds within the line give the effect of the heaving of a boat through a rolling swell.

More pleasing, probably because apparently not so sought for, are the following two lines from Keats's *Ode to Autumn*, in which the rhythm of the lines, and in particular the sound of the word *oozings* and the following phrase *hours by hours*, give particular reinforcement to the sense.

> Or by a cyder-press, with patient look,
> Thou watchest the last oozings, hours by hours.

It has often been observed that the denunciatory organ-roll of Milton's sonnet *On the Late Massacre in Piedmont* is built up on the open 'O' sound. A close study of the sonnet will show that other vowel and some consonantal sounds are harmonized with the open 'O' sounds to produce the peculiar tone of prophetic denunciation.

> Avenge, O Lord! Thy slaughter'd saints, whose bones
> Lie scatter'd on the Alpine mountains cold;
> Even them who kept Thy truth so pure of old
> When all our fathers worshipt stocks and stones,
>
> Forget not: In Thy book record their groans
> Who were Thy sheep, and in their ancient fold
> Slain by the bloody Piemontese, that roll'd
> Mother with infant down the rocks. Their moans
>
> The vales redoubled to the hills, and they
> To Heaven. Their martyr'd blood and ashes sow
> O'er all the Italian fields, where still doth sway
>
> The triple Tyrant: that from these may grow
> A hundred-fold, who, having learnt Thy way,
> Early may fly the Babylonian woe.

Higher in fine musical quality must rank the following passage from Coleridge's *Ancient Mariner*, in which there is an undertone of water-music, reaching a quiet culmination in the last line, surely one of the finest onomatopoeic effects in English poetry, because one of the subtlest and least obtrusive.

It ceased; yet still the sails made on
A pleasant noise till noon,
A noise like of a hidden brook
In the leafy month of June,
That to the sleeping woods all night
Singeth a quiet tune.

It would take up too much space to analyse this passage *fully*. Readers may find it particularly helpful to study the effect of the words containing 'sibilant' sounds, and of the musical undercurrent of the words 'noon', 'June', 'tune'.

CHAPTER V

IMAGERY

In Chapter III we have touched incidentally on imagery, especially Shakespearean imagery. In this chapter it is proposed to examine the subject more closely, and in greater detail. The use of imagery really turns on the perception of likeness in difference and difference in likeness. Every common object, every idea has a connotation as wide as the number of people who can apprehend the object or comprehend the idea. That is why language can express so little with absolute definition, and yet imply so much. The word *stone*, for example, to one person implies an object which improves or lowers the value of his land, to another the material of which his house is made, to another the missile with which David slew Goliath, to another the jewel adorning the person of a friend, to another a distressing and painful malady, to another the essential characteristics of a particular sea-shore. Even those to whom the word primarily suggests 'pebble' see in their mind's eye something quite different when the word is mentioned. To one appears an image of a strangely marked object glistening in the receding tide, to another a whitish or dark irregular shaped object turned over by the garden rake, to another unpleasant objects infinitely varied in shape, colour, size, and sharpness which impede his progress from his bathing tent to the water, to yet another particular *stones* to which Tennyson refers in the following lines from *The Princess.*

And all her thoughts as fair within her eyes,
As bottom agates seen to wave and float
In crystal currents of clear morning seas.

But just as the applications of the word in the sense of concrete and easily recognizable objects and materials are varied, so too are the figurative applications of the word. This point may easily be grasped when we remember that the simplest figure of speech, the 'simile', implies a comparison between two objects on different planes of thought, by virtue of some similarity which may be slight, or accidental, or temporary, valid in the particular circumstances only, stressing for the occasion some quality which may be one of the least—or most—important in the connotation of the object concerned. So with metaphor, which is merely a simile carried a stage further, a simile without the directly comparing word 'like' or 'as'. Thus when in Shakespeare's *Twelfth Night*, the Lady Olivia says

I have said too much unto a heart of stone,
And laid mine honour too unchary out.

the figure implies a physical characteristic of *stone*, its hardness, and a moral quality of *heart*, the word being used, not with strict application to the physical organ, but with application to the human personality. And yet the appropriateness of the metaphor in this instance depends to some extent on a vague association of ideas between the physical human heart and the ideas of softness and hardness, which in their turn are associated with the idea of granting or denying a petition.

If, on the other hand, a shot bird, or a damaged aeroplane, is said to drop like a stone, it is not the idea of hardness which is the basis of comparison.

In the sonnet beginning

> Since brass, nor stone, nor earth, nor boundless sea
> But sad mortality o'ersways their power,

the word *stone* is used partly in its literal, material sense, and partly in a general and abstract sense implying qualities of hardness and durability.

In the lines in Milton's sonnet *On the Late Massacre in Piedmont*

> Even them who kept thy Truth so pure of old,
> When all our fathers worshipt stocks and stones,
> Forget not:

it is obvious that the meaning of the word *stone* is even further removed from its mere literal, material sense. It starts off, it is true, from the meaning of an object made of stone, but the mind is directed more to the purpose of the object made of stone, its function as an idol worshipped by the superstitious.

It would be impossible, in a single chapter, to analyse fully the different ways in which imagery is used by poets, or even to illustrate adequately the varying degrees of emotional intensity which figurative language is capable of provoking. By taking specific examples we may get some idea of the nature and range and depth of poetic imagery. Let us consider the following passages:

> 1. O my Luve's like a red, red rose
> That's newly sprung in June:
> O my Luve's like the melodie
> That's sweetly play'd in tune.

1. In the first passage Burns's simile of the rose is a simple one, based on an obvious physical comparison. The

youthful and vigorous beauty of the beloved object suggests naturally and spontaneously the red freshness of an opening rose. A red rose suggests the full-blooded vitality of young love. 'My luve' is regarded in its dual capacity as the passion of the lovers and the poet's 'luve' herself. *It* and *she* are fresh, vital, and elemental. In the second two lines, the word 'luve' refers more precisely not merely to the object of 'luve' but to 'luve' itself, to the harmony of the lovers. There is no apparent subtlety of conception in the simile, but a spontaneous appropriateness. It seems inevitable that one should regard such love in such a way.

2. A face that's best
By its own beauty drest,
And can alone commend the rest:

A face made up
Out of no other shop
Than what Nature's white hand sets ope.

2. In the second passage, Crashaw's first metaphor, though not particularly harsh and strained, is certainly not a natural one, not based on a spontaneous comparison. 'Drest' suggests something external, applied to the face; it is more appropriate to an artificial made-up beauty than to natural beauty. The metaphor 'drest' is in fact dictated by an implied comparison in the next stanza between natural beauty and beauty derived from the shop. As a metaphor for natural beauty 'drest' is a little forced and inappropriate. The metaphor of the 'shop that Nature's white hand sets ope' is decidedly strained and unnatural, though it is suggested by the metaphor in the previous stanza. There is a harmony in the *relation* between the two metaphors, though each in varying degrees seems forced. The first metaphor is almost a *conceit*, the second is clearly one. The two stanzas and indeed the whole poem from which they are taken are fanci-

ful, and, though pleasing in a way, are not so emotionally satisfying as the first passage.

3. It is a beauteous evening, calm and free;
 The holy time is quiet as a Nun
 Breathless with adoration; the broad sun
Is sinking down in its tranquillity;

3. The imagery in this passage, the first four lines of one of Wordsworth's finest sonnets, is arresting in its beauty. The reader's first feeling of surprise at the comparison quickly disappears as the appropriateness of the image and the subsequent elaboration becomes progressively clear. The image of the nun bowed motionless in silent adoration is perfectly harmonized with the elements in the natural scene, the mystic hush of Nature as the sun, too, sinks low. Not only the images but the movement of the lines and the vowel and consonantal sounds are in complete harmony.

4. Down the road someone is practising scales,
The notes like little fishes vanish with a wink of tails.

4. The conceit in this passage is as recondite as any of Donne's, and just as satisfying to the imagination as the best of his, but more pleasing, with an element of charm which his seldom if ever have. The element of oddness is sufficiently marked to surprise and amuse, but too lightly pleasing to shock the mind with a sense of the grotesque. The word 'wink' in the final phrase turns an odd conceit 'notes like little fishes' into a triumph of humorous fancy. The couplet invites careful comparison with the central simile or conceit in passage 7.

5. And now the earth they had spurned rose up against them in anger,
Tier upon tier it towered, the terrible Apennines:
No sanctuary there for wings, not flares nor landing-lines,
No hope of floor and hangar.

Yet those ice-tipped spears that disputed the passage set spurs
To their two hundred and forty horse power; grimly they gained
Altitude, though the hand of heaven was heavy upon them,
The downdraught from the mountains: though desperate eddies spun them
Like a coin, yet unkindly tossed their luck came uppermost
And mastery remained.

5. In this passage, from C. Day Lewis's poem *The Flight*, no particular image impresses the reader with a sense of particular brilliance or imaginative insight. The power of the imagery lies rather in its cumulative effect on the mind. Occasionally it verges on the conceit, but nowhere is grotesque or even whimsical. The figure of the avenging earth is sustained in the first two lines. In the third line there is a change of figure. The earth is compared no longer with a *person*, but with a *place*. In the fifth there is a return to the original figure, the notion of the avenging earth. The mountains now suggest 'ice-tipped spears' confronting the aviators, and 'disputing their passage'. That suggests a piece of word-play in the reference to the '*spurs*' urging on their 'two hundred and forty *horse* power'. This is again followed by a reversion to the dominant image of avenging power 'the hand of heaven', 'the downdraught from the mountains'. The imagery in lines 8–9 is bold, but follows quite naturally from the context, and is hardly a conceit. The whole passage, in fact, affords a good example of the power of bold metaphor in vigorous narrative.

6. Her gentlewomen, like the Nereides,
So many mermaids, tended her i' the eyes,

And made their bends adornings: at the helm
A seeming mermaid steers: the silken tackle
Swell with the touches of those flower-soft hands,
That yarely frame the office. From the barge
A strange invisible perfume hits the sense
Of the adjacent wharfs. The city cast
Her people out upon her; and Antony,
Enthroned i' the market-place, did sit alone,
Whistling to the air.

6. Enobarbus, in Shakespeare's *Antony and Cleopatra*, is telling Agrippa about Cleopatra's progress up the river Cydnus in a barge. The voluptuous beauty of the Queen, and its effect on the impressionable Antony is described in this and the previous passage in the scene in a succession of images full of delicate fancy. The simile of the Nereides, with the amplification 'so many mermaids', suggests the sinuous charm of the Queen's female attendants, and the following phrase 'made their bends adornings' conveys an impression that these nymphs were almost part of the curving lines of the boat as it glides through the water. Appropriate to the general character of the scene are the epithets 'silken', 'flower-soft'. Vigorous metaphors might be thought out of place in such a pattern of filigree fancy, but the concrete images in the next two sentences, the reference to the perfume that 'hits the sense' of the adjacent wharfs, and that to the surging welcome given to Cleopatra, 'the city cast her people out upon her', though in vivid contrast to the daintiness of the preceding images, do not in any way clash with them.

7. Our two souls therefore, which are one,
Though I must go, endure not yet
A breach, but an expansion,
Like gold to airy thinness beat.

If they be two, they are two so
  As stiff twin compasses are two,
Thy soul, the fix'd foot, makes no show
  To move, but doth, if th'other do.

And though it in the centre sit,
  Yet when the other far doth roam,
It leans and hearkens after it,
  And grows erect as that comes home.

Such wilt thou be to me, who must
  Like th'other foot obliquely run,
Thy firmness makes my circle just,
  And makes me end where I begun.

7. In the fourth example we have a conceit which like others of Donne pleases as well as amuses the fancy. In this passage, however, the comparison between the pair of friends and the pair of compasses, though it has some superficial appropriateness, seems too mechanical and odd to do more than interest by its strangeness. It has a purely intellectual validity, and that a slight one. It lacks charm. It tickles the fancy without capturing and delighting the imagination. There is no real and compelling truth in the comparison, as can be seen if we examine closely the details.

8. His pupil age
Man-enter'd thus, he waxed like a sea;
And, in the brunt of seventeen battles since,
He lurch'd all swords of the garland. For this last,
Before and in Corioli, let me say,
I cannot speak him home: he stopp'd the fliers;
And by his rare example made the coward
Turn terror into sport; as weeds before
A vessel under sail, so men obey'd,
And fell below his stem: his sword, death's stamp,

Where it did mark, it took; from face to foot
He was a thing of blood, whose every motion
Was timed with dying cries: alone he enter'd
The mortal gate of the city, which he painted
With shunless destiny;

8. This passage is singular not only because of the vigour of its figurative language but because of its compression. In places the meaning is obscure because of this. These are occasional characteristics of Shakespeare's latest poetic style. At times this compression makes his language appear clumsy and ugly. For example, the opening image 'His pupil age man-entered thus', more a simple comparison than a metaphor, is an ugly if vigorous way of saying that in mere boyhood he behaved as bravely as a full-grown man. 'As weeds before a vessel under sail', on the other hand, is a picturesque and highly appropriate figure. It affords a clear mental image of the yielding of lesser men before the onrush of a great warrior, like weeds falling back from the bows of a ship. In the tenth line the metaphor is blurred. A sword cannot be clearly visualized as stamping death upon the fallen. In lines twelve to fifteen, the figurative language, marked by extreme vividness and vigour as well as compression, is not confined to simile and metaphor. In the phrase 'dying cries', 'dying' is an instance of *transferred epithet*. The phrase means 'cries of dying men'. The use of this figure heightens the effect. In lines fourteen to fifteen the language is more compressed than in any other part of the passage. 'Mortal gate' suggests a confined space heaped with the bodies of those who have found death there, 'painted' is a vivid image suggesting that the gate is thickly overlaid with the blood of men. 'Shunless destiny' is an instance of double metonymy, 'destiny' standing for the death which overtook them, and the blood which is the outward sign of death. 'Painted with

shunless destiny' means, then, 'covered thick with the blood the victims shed as the token of the death which was their fate'.

9. Come, fill the Cup, and in the Fire of Spring
The Winter Garment of Repentance fling:
  The Bird of Time has but a little way
To fly—and Lo! the Bird is on the Wing.

9. In passage nine Fitzgerald's figurative language is picturesque but touched with conventionality. 'Fill the cup', though it is partly to be taken in its literal sense, also suggests pleasure generally. 'Spring' is the conventional metaphor for 'Youth', as 'Fire' is for the attributes of Youth. In the next line the metaphorical expression is more original. 'Repentance' as a cloak for sins of pleasure is more appropriate to the 'Winter' of life than to its spring. 'Winter' is, of course, a conventional metaphor for old age, though its association with 'Garment of Repentance' gives the whole conception the stamp of originality. Though the personification of Time is a frequent convention in poetry, it is usually likened to an old man. The comparison to a 'Bird on the Wing' is distinctive.

10. Had I but died an hour before this chance,
I had lived a blessed time; for from this instant
There's nothing serious in mortality:
All is but toys: renown and grace is dead;
The wine of life is drawn, and the mere lees
Is left this vault to brag of.

10. In the tenth passage Macbeth is hypocritically lamenting the death of King Duncan, whom he has murdered. In the fourth line of the passage 'toys' is an obvious conventional figure for the trivialities of life. 'Renown' and 'Grace' are partly personified. In the last two lines, however, the metaphors have a peculiarly Shakespearian ring. They have

partly an abstract, partly a concrete suggestiveness. As wine cheers the heart of men, so King Duncan cheers the society in which he lives. Now that he is dead, says Macbeth, with hypocritical exaggeration of language, those left are but as the 'lees', the worthless residue. But Duncan, 'his silver skin laced with his golden blood', has been stabbed to death. His blood, symbol of life and vigour, has been drained from his body; his mere clay is all that is left for the world to claim as its own. This use of metaphor with both an abstract and a concrete application is typical of Shakespearian imagery.

NOTE. Some of these comments may be, probably are, valid for most readers of poetry, some of them may be valid for a few, some of them valid for none but the writer of these notes. Read the passages and compare your own impressions and opinions with those expressed above.

EXERCISE ON CHAPTERS III AND V

Examine critically the language and imagery of each of the following passages of poetry:

1. Come, Sleep: O Sleep! the certain knot of peace,
The baiting-place of wit, the balm of woe,
The poor man's wealth, the prisoner's release,
Th'indifferent judge between the high and low;

With shield of proof shield me from out the prease
Of those fierce darts Despair at me doth throw:
O make in me those civil wars to cease;
I will good tribute pay, if thou do so.

Take thou of me smooth pillows, sweetest bed,
A chamber deaf of noise and blind of light,
A rosy garland and a weary head:
And if these things, as being thine in right,

Move not thy heavy grace, thou shalt in me,
Livelier than elsewhere, Stella's image see.

SIR PHILIP SIDNEY

2. The fair breeze blew, the white foam flew,
The furrow followed free;
We were the first that ever burst
Into that silent sea.

Down dropt the breeze, the sails dropt down,
'Twas sad as sad could be;
And we did speak only to break
The silence of the sea!

All in a hot and copper sky,
The bloody Sun, at noon,
Right up above the mast did stand,
No bigger than the Moon.

Day after day, day after day,
We stuck, nor breath nor motion;
As idle as a painted ship
Upon a painted ocean.

Water, water, everywhere,
And all the boards did shrink;
Water, water, everywhere
Nor any drop to drink.

The very deep did rot: O Christ!
That ever this should be!
Yea, slimy things did crawl with legs
Upon the slimy sea.

S. T. COLERIDGE

3. *Juliet.* Wilt thou be gone? It is not yet near day:
It was the nightingale, and not the lark,
That pierced the fearful hollow of thine ear;
Believe me, love, it was the nightingale.
Romeo. It was the lark, the herald of the morn,
No nightingale: look, love, what envious streaks
Do lace the severing clouds in yonder east:
Night's candles are burnt out, and jocund day
Stands tiptoe on the misty mountain tops:
I must be gone and live, or stay and die.

W. SHAKESPEARE

4. But O, my muse, what numbers wilt thou find
To sing the furious troops in battle join'd!
Methinks I hear the drum's tumultuous sound,
The victor's shouts and dying groans confound,
The dreadful burst of cannon rend the skies,
And all the thunder of the battle rise.
'Twas then great Marlbro's mighty soul was prov'd,
That, in the shock of charging hosts unmov'd,
Amidst confusion, horror, and despair,
Examin'd all the dreadful scenes of war;
In peaceful thought the field of death survey'd,
To fainting squadrons sent the timely aid,
Inspir'd repuls'd battalions to engage,
And taught the doubtful battle where to rage.
So when an angel by divine command
With rising tempests shakes a guilty land,
Such as of late o'er pale Britannia past,
Calm and serene he drives the furious blast;
And pleas'd th'Almighty's orders to perform,
Rides in the whirlwind, and directs the storm.

J. ADDISON

5. This fellow pecks up wit as pigeons pease,
And utters it again when God doth please:
He is wit's pedler, and retails his wares
At wakes and wassails, meetings, markets, fairs;
And we that sell by gross, the Lord doth know,
Have not the grace to grace it with such show.
This gallant pins the wenches on his sleeve;
Had he been Adam, he had tempted Eve;
A' can carve too, and lisp; why this is he
That kiss'd his hand away in courtesy;
This is the ape of form, monsieur the nice,
That, when he plays at tables, chides the dice
In honourable terms: nay, he can sing
A mean most meanly; and in ushering,
Mend him who can: the ladies call him sweet;
The stairs, as he treads on them, kiss his feet:
This is the flower that smiles on every one,
To show his teeth as white as whale's bone.

W. SHAKESPEARE

6. Blest infant bud, whose blossom-life
Did only look about, and fall
Wearied out in a harmless strife
Of tears, and milk, the food of all;

Sweetly didst thou expire: thy soul
Flew home unstain'd by his new kin;
For ere thou knew'st how to be foul,
Death wean'd thee from the world, and sin.

Softly rest all thy virgin-crumbs
Lapt in the sweets of thy young breath,
Expecting till thy Saviour comes
To dress them, and unswaddle death!

HENRY VAUGHAN

7. To be, or not to be: that is the question:
Whether 'tis nobler in the mind to suffer
The slings and arrows of outrageous fortune,
Or to take arms against a sea of troubles,
And by opposing end them. To die: to sleep;
No more; and by a sleep to say we end
The heart-ache, and the thousand natural shocks
That flesh is heir to, 'tis a consummation
Devoutly to be wish'd. To die, to sleep;
To sleep: perchance to dream: ay, there 's the rub;
For in that sleep of death what dreams may come,
When we have shuffled off this mortal coil,
Must give us pause: there 's the respect
That makes calamity of so long life;
For who would bear the whips and scorns of time,
The oppressor's wrong, the proud man's contumely,
The pangs of despised love, the law's delay,
The insolence of office, and the spurns
That patient merit of the unworthy takes,
When he himself might his quietus make
With a bare bodkin? who would fardels bear,
To grunt and sweat under a weary life,
But that the dread of something after death,
The undiscover'd country from whose bourn
No traveller returns, puzzles the will,
And makes us rather bear those ills we have
Than fly to others that we know not of?

Thus conscience does make cowards of us all,
And thus the native hue of resolution
Is sicklied o'er with the pale cast of thought,
And enterprises of great pitch and moment
With this regard their currents turn awry
And lose the name of action. W. SHAKESPEARE

8. Weep no more, woeful shepherds, weep no more,
For Lycidas your sorrow is not dead,
Sunk though he be beneath the wat'ry floor;
So sinks the daystar in the ocean bed,
And yet anon repairs his drooping head,
And tricks his beams, and with new-spangled ore
Flames in the forehead of the morning sky:
So Lycidas sunk low, but mounted high,
Through the dear might of Him that walk'd the waves;
Where, other groves and other streams along,
With nectar pure his oozy locks he laves,
And hears the unexpressive nuptial song,
In the blest kingdoms meek of joy and love.
There entertain him all the saints above,
In solemn troops and sweet societies,
That sing, and singing in their glory move,
And wipe the tears for ever from his eyes.
Now, Lycidas, the shepherds weep no more;
Henceforth thou art the genius of the shore,
In thy large recompense, and shalt be good
To all that wander in that perilous flood
Thus sang the uncouth swain to the oaks and rills,
While the still morn went out with sandals grey;
He touch'd the tender stops of various quills,
With eager thought warbling his Doric lay:
And now the sun had stretch'd out all the hills,
And now was dropt into the western bay:
At last he rose, and twitch'd his mantle blue:
To-morrow to fresh woods, and pastures new.

JOHN MILTON

9. Now Time's Andromeda on this rock rude,
With not her either beauty's equal or
Her injury's, looks off by both horns of shore,
Her flower, her piece of being, doomed dragon's food.

Time past she has been attempted and pursued
By many blows and banes; but now hears roar
A wilder beast from West than all were, more
Rife in her wrongs, more lawless, and more lewd.

Her Perseus linger and leave her to her extremes?—
Pillowy air he treads a time and hangs
His thoughts on her, forsaken that she seems,
All while her patience, morselled into pangs,
Mounts; then to alight disarming, no one dreams,
With Gorgon's gear and barebill, thongs and fangs.

GERARD MANLEY HOPKINS

10. We talk'd with open heart, and tongue
Affectionate and true,
A pair of Friends, though I was young,
And Matthew seventy-two.

We lay beneath a spreading-oak,
Beside a mossy seat;
And from the turf a fountain broke
And gurgled at our feet.

'Now, Matthew!' said I, 'let us match
This water's pleasant tune
With some old Border-song, or Catch
That suits a summer's noon;

'Or of the Church-clock and the chimes
Sing here beneath the shade
That half-mad thing of witty rhymes
Which you last April made!'

In silence Matthew lay, and eyed
The spring beneath the tree;
And thus the dear old man replied,
The gray hair'd man of glee:

'No check, no stay, this Streamlet fears,
Now merrily it goes!
'Twill murmur on a thousand years
And flow as now it flows.

'And here, on this delightful day,
I cannot choose but think
How oft, a vigorous Man, I lay
Beside this Fountain's brink.

'My eyes are dim with childish tears,
My heart is idly stirr'd,
For the same sound is in my ears
Which in those days I heard.

'Thus fares it still in our decay:
And yet the wiser mind
Mourns less for what Age takes away,
Than what it leaves behind.'

W. WORDSWORTH

11. At sixteen years,
When Tarquin made a head for Rome, he fought
Beyond the mark of others: our then dictator,
Whom with all praise I point at, saw him fight,
When with his Amazonian chin he drove
The bristled lips before him: he bestrid.
An o'erpress'd Roman, and i' the consul's view
Slew three opposers: Tarquin's self he met,
And struck him on his knee: in that day's feats,
When he might act the woman in the scene,
He proved best man i' the field, and for his meed
Was brow-bound with the oak. His pupil age
Man-enter'd thus, he waxed like a sea;
And, in the brunt of seventeen battles since,
He lurch'd all swords of the garland. For this last,
Before and in Corioli, let me say,
I cannot speak him home: he stopp'd the fliers;
And by his rare example made the coward
Turn terror into sport: as weeds before
A vessel under sail, so men obey'd
And fell below his stem: his sword, death's stamp,
Where it did mark, it took; from face to foot
He was a thing of blood, whose every motion
Was timed with dying cries: alone he enter'd
The mortal gate of the city, which he painted
With shunless destiny.

W. SHAKESPEARE

12. Far far from gusty waves, these children's faces
Like rootless weeds the torn hair round their paleness;
The tall girl with her weighed-down head; the paper-
seeming boy with rat's eyes; the stunted unlucky heir
Of twisted bones, reciting a father's gnarled disease,
His lesson from his desk. At back of the dim class
One unnoted, mild and young: his eyes live in a dream
Of squirrel's game, in tree room, other than this.

On sour cream walls, donations; Shakespeare's head
Cloudless at dawn, civilized dome riding all cities;
Belled, flowery, Tyrolese valley; open-handed map
Awarding the explicit world, of every name but here.
To few, too few, these are real windows: world and words
and waving
Leaves, to heal. For these young lives, guilty and dangerous
Is fantasy of travel. Surely, Shakespeare is wicked

To lives that wryly turn, under the structural Lie,
Toward smiles or hate? Amongst their heap, these children
Wear skins peeped through by bones, and spectacles of steel
With mended glass, like bottle bits in slag.
Tyrol is wicked; map's promising a fable:
All of their time and space are foggy slum,
So blot their maps with slums as big as doom.

Unless, dowager, governor, these pictures, in a room
Columned above childishness, like our day's future drift
Of smoke concealing war, are voices shouting
O that beauty has words and works which break
Through coloured walls and towers. The children stand
As in a climbing mountain train. This lesson illustrates
The world green in their many valleys beneath:
The total summer heavy with their flowers.

STEPHEN SPENDER

13. *Isabella.* Could great men thunder
As Jove himself does, Jove would ne'er be quiet,
For every pelting, petty officer
Would use his heaven for thunder.
Nothing but thunder! Merciful Heaven,
Thou rather with thy sharp and sulphurous bolt

Split'st the unwedgeable and gnarled oak
Than the soft myrtle: but man, proud man,
Drest in a little brief authority,
Most ignorant of what he's most assured,
His glassy essence, like an angry ape,
Plays such fantastic tricks before high heaven
As make the angels weep; who, with our spleens,
Would all themselves laugh mortal.

WILLIAM SHAKESPEARE

14. In the downhill of life, when I find I'm declining
  May my fate no less fortunate be
Than a snug elbow-chair will afford for reclining,
  And a cot that o'erlooks the wide sea;
With an ambling pad-pony to pace o'er the lawn,
  While I carol away idle sorrow,
And blithe as the lark that each day hails the dawn
  Look forward with hope for Tomorrow.

With a porch at my door, both for shelter and shade too,
  As the sunshine or rain may prevail;
And a small spot of ground for the use of the spade too,
  With a barn for the use of the flail:
A cow for my dairy, a dog for my game,
  And a purse when a friend wants to borrow;
I'll envy no Nabob his riches or fame,
  Or what honours may wait him Tomorrow.

And when I at last must throw off this frail covering
  Which I've worn for three-score years and ten,
On the brink of the grave I'll not seek to keep hov'ring,
  Nor my thread wish to spin o'er again:
But my face in the glass I'll serenely survey,
  And with smiles count each wrinkle and furrow;
As this old worn-out stuff, which is thread-bare Today,
  May become Everlasting Tomorrow.

J. COLLINS

15. Now, my fair'st friend,
I would I had some flowers o' the spring that might
Become your time of day; and yours, and yours,
That wear upon your virgin branches yet

Your maidenheads growing: O Proserpina,
For the flowers now, that frighted thou let'st fall
From Dis's waggon! daffodils,
That come before the swallow dares, and take
The winds of March with beauty; violets dim,
But sweeter than the lids of Juno's eyes
Or Cytherea's breath; pale primroses,
That die unmarried, ere they can behold
Bright Phoebus in his strength, a malady
Most incident to maids; bold oxlips and
The crown imperial; lilies of all kinds,
The flower-de-luce being one! O, these I lack,
To make you garlands of.

W. SHAKESPEARE

16. She dwelt among the untrodden ways
Beside the springs of Dove;
A maid whom there were none to praise,
And very few to love.

A violet by a mossy stone
Half hidden from the eye!
—Fair as a star, when only one
Is shining in the sky.

She lived unknown, and few could know
When Lucy ceased to be;
But she is in her grave, and, oh,
The difference to me!

W. WORDSWORTH

17. 'Tis loss to trust a tomb with such a guest,
Or to confine her in a marble chest.
Alas! what's marble, jet, or porphyry,
Prized with the chrysolite of either eye,
Or with those pearls and rubies which she was?
Join the two Indies in one tomb, 'tis glass;
And so is all, to her materials,
Though every inch were ten Escurials;
Yet she's demolish'd; can we keep her then
In works of hands, or of the wits of men?
Can these memorials, rags of paper, give
Life to that name, by which name they must live?

Sickly, alas! short-lived, abortive be
Those carcase verses, whose soul is not she;
And can she, who no longer would be she,
Being such a tabernacle stoop to be
In paper wrapp'd; or when she would not lie
In such an house, dwell in an elegy?
But 'tis no matter; we may well allow
Verse to live so long as the world will now,
For her death wounded it. The world contains
Princes for arms, and counsellors for brains,
Lawyers for tongues, divines for hearts, and more,
The rich for stomachs, and for backs the poor;
The officers for hands, merchants for feet,
By which remote and distant countries meet;
But those fine spirits, which do tune and set
This organ, are those pieces which beget
Wonder and love; and these were she; and she
Being spent, the world must needs decrepit be.

JOHN DONNE

18. Of all the girls that are so smart
There's none like pretty Sally;
She is the darling of my heart,
And she lives in our alley.
There is no lady in the land
Is half so sweet as Sally;
She is the darling of my heart,
And she lives in our alley.

Her father he makes cabbage-nets
And through the streets does cry 'em;
Her mother she sells laces long
To such as please to buy 'em:
But sure such folks could ne'er beget
So sweet a girl as Sally!
She is the darling of my heart,
And she lives in our alley.

When she is by, I leave my work,
I love her so sincerely;
My master comes like any Turk,
And bangs me most severely—

But let him bang his bellyful,
  I'll bear it all for Sally;
She is the darling of my heart,
  And she lives in our alley.

19. Pure faith indeed—you know not what you ask!
Naked belief in God the Omnipotent,
Omniscient, Omnipresent, sears too much
The sense of conscious creatures to be borne.
It were the seeing him, no flesh shall dare.
Some think, Creation 's meant to show him forth:
I say, it's meant to hide him all it can,
And that's what all the blessed Evil 's for.
Its use in time is to environ us,
Our breath, our drop of dew, with shield enough
Against that sight till we can bear its stress.
Under a vertical sun, the exposed brain
And lidless eye and disemprisoned heart
Less certainly would wither up at once
Than mind, confronted with the truth of Him.
But time and earth case-harden us to live;
The feeblest sense is trusted most; the child
Feels God a moment, ichors o'er the place,
Plays on and grows to be a man like us.
With me, faith means perpetual unbelief
Kept quiet like the snake 'neath Michael's foot
Who stands calm just because he feels it writhe.
Or, if that's too ambitious,—here 's my box—
I need the excitation of a pinch
Threatening the torpor of the inside-nose
Nigh on the imminent sneeze that never comes.
'Leave it in peace' advise the simple folk—
Make it aware of peace by itching-fits,
Say I—let doubt occasion still more faith!

ROBERT BROWNING

20. He walks the world with mountains in his breast,
And holds the hiltless wind in vassalage.
Transtellar spaces are his fields of quiet,
Eternity his spirit's ambassage.

The uneared acre of the firmaments
Under his hungry harrow, yields increase.
While, from the threshold of dim continents
They beckon him, who bears the stars in lease.

And yet he is a thane of foreigners,
On sapphire throned, but in an unkinged house,
Arrased with honours, broidered in gold sheen—
A palace in a town of sepulchres.
Voices he hears, but knows not what they mean,
His own to him the most mysterious.

F. V. BRANFORD

CHAPTER VI

'SWING'

THE *vague* experience of pleasure from rhythm is one of the earliest evidences of critical appreciation in children. Even when we are older, and experience delight in poetry, we can often do little more than say 'It goes with a swing'. Similarly we express our disapproval of a particular poem by saying that it has no swing. 'Swing' is indeed as potent to stimulate pleasure in poetry as it is in modern types of music. We shall not, at this stage, if ever, be able to analyse fully what we mean by 'swing', but we can find out something of what constitutes 'swing' or rhythm in poetry.

Let us begin with the more formal approach to the subject. A line of English poetry is, or was said to be, made up of so many feet, each consisting of one or more stressed syllables and one or more unstressed syllables. For example, many English poems are made up of lines containing five feet. In each foot the even-numbered syllables are stressed, and the odd-numbered syllables are unstressed. The following stanza from Gray's *Elegy Written In A Country Churchyard* contains four such lines. A foot in which the even-numbered syllable is stressed is called an iambic foot.

The cur|few tolls | the knell | of part|ing day,
The low|ing herd | winds slow|ly o'er | the lea,
The plough|man home|ward plods | his wear|y way,
And leaves | the world | to dark|ness, and | to me

The even-numbered, stressed syllables are indicated by the *grave* accent. It will be noted that in the fourth foot of the fourth line the stressed syllable is marked with an acute accent. That is merely because the word 'and' in this line does not bear so strong a stress as the other stressed syllables. In the third foot of the second line the syllable 'slow-' in 'slowly' bears a strong stress; the word 'winds', however, is also stressed, and is hence marked with a grave accent.

Actually it is very rare to find verse so regularly iambic as that in Gray's *Elegy*. The succession of iambic feet is varied by occasional feet of another type. Even in Gray's *Elegy*, one of the most regular of all poems, where the almost unbroken succession of iambic feet suggests by the very sequence the monotonous march of Death, there are occasional feet that are not iambic. In the second stanza of the poem,

Now fades | the glimm|ering land|scape on | the sight,
And all | the air | a sol|emn still|ness holds,
Save where | the bee|tle wheels | his dron|ing flight,
And drow|sy tink|lings lull | the dist|ant folds

if the poem is read naturally, both syllables in the first foot of lines one and three must be given equal or almost equal stress. So, too, in the third stanza,

Save that | from yon|der ivy|-man|tled tower
The mop|ing owl | does to | the moon | complain.

In the first foot of the first line both syllables are stressed, though the second is only lightly stressed. In the third foot of the second line the first syllable is stressed.

Normally, even in poetry where the predominant rhythm is iambic there is considerable variation of stress. Otherwise intolerable monotony would be the result. In Gray's *Elegy*, as we have seen, regularity of rhythm is conditioned by the subject and spirit of the poem, and though, in a sense, the result is a certain degree of monotony, that monotony is rather pleasing. Now read slowly the following poem, without attempting to mark off the feet, and indicate with a grave accent each syllable which clearly bears a strong stress. Then read through again, and mark with an acute accent each syllable bearing a lighter stress,

Like as | the waves | make towards | the pebb|led shore,
  So do | our min|utes hast|en to | their end;
Each chang|ing place | with that | which goes | before,
  In se|quent toil | all for|wards do | contend.

Nativ|ity, | once in | the main | of light,
  Crawls to | matur|ity, | wherewith | being crown'd,
Crooked | eclips|es 'gainst | his glor|y fight,
  And Time | that gave | doth now | his gift | confound.

Time doth | transfix | the flour|ish set | on youth,
  And delves | the par|allels | on beau|ty's brow;
Feeds on | the rar|ities | of nat|ure's truth,
  And noth|ing stands | but for | his scythe | to mow:

And yet, | to times | in hope, | my verse | shall stand
Praising | thy worth, | despite | his cru|el hand.

It will be seen that of the fourteen lines in this sonnet only two or three have five iambic feet. In all the others there is some variation. The first three lines and the last, for example, have each a spondee, a foot, that is, in which both syllables bear a strong stress. The second, fifth, sixth, tenth, and eleventh contain syllables with no strong stress, but a lighter stress. That is shown by the acute accent. The first, sixth, seventh, ninth, eleventh, twelfth, and fourteenth contain each a trochee, a foot in which the first syllable is stressed. If you read through the poem a third time stressing mechanically all the even-numbered syllables, passing lightly over the odd-numbered ones, you will see that the poem depends for its musical effect and meaning on this variation from the strictly regular iambic rhythm.

Now read through the following passage from Milton's *L'Allegro*, marking carefully the syllables on which the strong stress naturally falls:

Haste thee, Nymph, and bring with thee
Jest, and youthful jollity,
Quips, and cranks, and wanton wiles,
Nods, and becks, and wreathed smiles
Such as hang on Hebe's cheek,
And love to live in dimple sleek;
Sport that wrinkled care derides,
And Laughter holding both his sides.

In six of the eight lines the strong stress is on the odd-numbered syllables; there are usually seven syllables in the line and four strong stresses. The line thus contains three trochees, and ends with a stressed syllable. This is frequently called 'falling' rhythm. In two of the lines, the sixth and the eighth, the stress is on even-numbered syllables. In these lines, which contain eight syllables, there are four iambic feet. This kind of rhythm is called rising rhythm. Falling rhythm is also found in Robert Browning's poem *Home-thoughts, From The Sea.*

Nobly, nobly Cape Saint Vincent to the North-West died away;
Sunset ran, one glorious blood-red, reeking into Cadiz Bay;
Bluish mid the burning water, full in face Trafalgar lay;
In the dimmest North-East distance, dawned Gibraltar grand and grey;
'Here and there did England help me: how can I help England?'—say,
Whoso turns as I, this evening, turn to God to praise and pray,
While Jove's planet rises yonder, silent over Africa.

Each line, it will be seen, consists of seven trochees followed by a single accented syllable.

Read through the following short passages, and then mark the stresses. The first passage, it will be seen, contains feet consisting of a stressed syllable followed by two unstressed, the second contains feet consisting of two unstressed syllables followed by one stressed syllable. A foot consisting of a stressed syllable followed by two unstressed is called a *dactyl*: the reverse of a dactyl is an *anapaest*. The first passage has alternate lines consisting respectively of two dactyls and a dactyl followed by a trochee. In the second the lines consist of two anapaests.

1. Pibroch of | Donuil Dhu,
Pibroch of | Donuil,
Wake thy wild | voice anew,
Summon Clan | Conuil.
Come away, | come away,
Hark to the | summons!
Come in your | war-array,
Gentles and | commons.

2. Over hill, | over dale,
Thorough bush, | thorough brier,
Over park, | over pale,
Thorough flood, | thorough fire.

In the following two short passages from Coleridge's *Christabel*, iambs, trochees, dactyls, and anapaests, the four common types of metrical foot used in English poetry, will be found. It has also three spondees, or feet containing two strongly stressed syllables. Coleridge was very fond of experimenting with metre, and frequently varies the rhythm in both *Christabel* and *The Ancient Mariner* in this way:

The lovely lady, Christabel,
Whom her father loves so well,
What makes her in the wood so late,
A furlong from the castle gate?

She had dreams all yesternight
Of her own betrothed knight;
And she in the midnight wood will pray
For the weal of her lover that's far away.

There is not wind enough to twirl
The one red leaf, the last of its clan,
That dances as often as dance it can,
Hanging so light, and hanging so high,
On the topmost twig that looks up at the sky.

It will now be interesting to see what varied effects poets produce by the employment of different kinds of metre, and what other means are associated with metre to produce these effects. First read carefully through the following passages, aloud if possible:

1. I sprang to the stirrup, and Joris, and he;
I galloped, Dirck galloped, we galloped all three;
'Good speed!' cried the watch, as the gate-bolts undrew;
'Speed!' echoed the wall to us galloping through;
Behind shut the postern, the lights sank to rest,
And into the midnight we galloped abreast.

Not a word to each other: we kept the great pace
Neck by neck, stride by stride, never changing our place;
I turned in my saddle and made its girths tight,
Then shortened each stirrup, and set the pique right,
Rebuckled the cheek-strap, chained slacker the bit,
Nor galloped less steadily Roland a whit.

ROBERT BROWNING: *How They Brought The Good News From Ghent to Aix.*

2. As I ride, as I ride,
With a full heart for my guide
So its tide rocks my side,
As I ride, as I ride,
That, as I were double-eyed,
He, in whom our Tribes confide,
Is descried, ways untried,
As I ride, as I ride.

ROBERT BROWNING: *Through The Metida To Abd-El-Kadr.*

3. They see the Heroes
Sitting in the dark ship
On the foamless, long-heaving,
Violet sea:
At sunset nearing
The Happy Islands.

MATTHEW ARNOLD: *The Strayed Reveller*

4. By the margin, willow-veiled,
Slide the heavy barges trail'd
By slow horses; and unhail'd
The shallop flitteth silken-sail'd
Skimming down to Camelot:

LORD TENNYSON: *The Lady of Shalott*

5. For most, I know, thou lov'st retired ground!
Thee, at the ferry, Oxford riders blithe,
Returning home on summer nights, have met
Crossing the stripling Thames at Bablock-hithe,
Trailing in the cool stream thy fingers wet,
As the punt's rope chops round;

MATTHEW ARNOLD: *The Scholar Gipsy*

If you read through the first stanza of the first passage, you will notice that each line has eleven syllables with four strong stresses, on the second, fifth, eighth and eleventh syllables respectively, the remaining syllables being either unstressed or lightly stressed. The line is thus made up of an iambus, followed by three anapaests. The second stanza is roughly the same, except that the first two lines have twelve syllables each, there being four anapaests to each line.

The general effect of this rollicking metre is to suggest the sound of galloping horses. The consonants in both the stressed and unstressed syllables contribute a good deal to the metallic *cloppety-clop* of the passage.

In the second passage five of the eight lines have six syllables each, three of them have seven. The six-syllabled lines have two strong stresses each, the seven-syllabled lines have three, though the first of them,

With a full heart for my guide

may be regarded as having two or three according to the way it is read. The general effect of the metre again is to echo the sense, and suggest the galloping of horses, though as the stress throughout is on the sound in the word *ride* the metallic *cloppety-clop* sound of the first passage is lacking.

Now read through the third passage, and then mark the strong stresses. In the first, fifth, and sixth lines it will be noticed there are two, on the second and fourth syllables respectively. In the fourth line there are two strong stresses, on the first and fourth syllables respectively. In the second line the first, fifth, and sixth syllables bear a strong stress, the first foot being a dactyl, with, as sometimes happens in dactylic verse, an extra unstressed syllable. In the third line the third, fifth, and sixth syllables bear strong stresses.

The passage may be scanned thus:

1.	∪ –	∪ –	∪
2.	– ∪ ∪ ∪	– –	
3.	∪ ∪ –	∪ –	– ∪
4.	– ∪	∪ –	
5.	∪ –	∪ –	∪
6.	∪ –	∪ –	∪

The first, third, fifth, and sixth lines have each a feminine ending.

This balancing of dactyl and anapaest, trochee and iambus gives a backwards and forwards roll to the verse, suggestive of the swell of the sea.

The first two lines of the fourth example contain three trochees and a single stressed syllable each. The third line is slightly, but significantly, varied, the first foot being a spondee, the rest of the line having the same stresses as the first two. The fourth line has four iambuses, the fifth two trochees and a dactyl. The effect of the spondee at the beginning of the third line, following the long stressed syllable in the words *slide*, *heavy*, *barges*, *trail'd*, is to accentuate the sense of laborious effort. Contrasted with this is the effect of the short vowels in the iambuses, trochees, and the single dactyl of the fourth and fifth lines, the difference between the movement of the heavy barges and that of the light shallop being thus made more impressive.

The first four lines of the fifth passage are mainly of normal rhythm, with an inverted stress in the first foot of the second and fourth lines. In the fifth line, after an opening inverted stress, there are two spondees, one in the third and one in the fourth foot. In the short sixth line there are two spondees, one in the second, and one in the third foot. The effect of these variations is to express by sound the suggestion of the retarded motion of the boat.

It is not intended in this chapter to illustrate at great length the use of metrical variation, and the effect of the interplay of metrical variation with such devices as alliteration and assonance. The following few examples must suffice.

1. Read carefully through the following stanza from Spenser's *Faerie Queene*, Book II, Canto XII:

> The joyous birdes, shrouded in chearefull shade
> Their notes unto the voice attempred sweet;
> Th' Angelicall soft trembling voyces made
> To th' instruments divine respondence meet
> The silver sounding instruments did meet
> With the base murmure of the waters fall;
> The waters fall with difference discreet,
> Now soft, now loud, unto the wind did call;
> The gentle warbling wind low answered to all.

It will be noticed that in four out of the nine lines there is no departure from regular iambic rhythm. In two of the remainder, lines one and two, there is an inverted stress in one foot. In line three the second foot has no strong stress, the third is a spondee. In line six there is an inverted stress, one foot is a spondee, and one foot has no strong stress. In line eight there are two spondees, in the first two feet, and an inverted stress in the third foot. Only in lines six and eight do these differences affect the metre markedly. These differences, great or small, are not in themselves sufficient to produce the stately, solemn, and often slow, languorous movement which is characteristic of Spenser's *Faerie Queene*. The linked rhymes and the final alexandrine have, of course, a good deal to do with that effect, which is also to some degree characteristic of Shelley's *Adonais* and Byron's *Childe Harold*, written, too, in the Spenserian stanza, which is the metrical form of *The Faerie Queene*. But in this particular stanza, and in much of *The Faerie Queene*, the effects noted are greatly helped by the harmonizing of vowel sounds, and by the constant alliteration, the repetition of the consonant 's'. In line six the weight of the stresses falls preponderantly on the spondee '*base mur*(mure)', suggesting, by sound, the huddling noise of the water. This is followed by a foot containing two unstressed syllables preceding the stress in the word *waters*. Thus the mind is first prepared for the *waters fall*, and then carried forward to it, the ear half consciously expecting it.

Now read through the following stanza from Canto IV of Byron's *Childe Harold:*

> The roar of waters!—from the headlong height
> Velino cleaves the wave-worn precipice;
> The fall of waters! rapid as the light
> The flashing mass foams shaking the abyss;
> The hell of waters! where they howl and hiss,
> And boil in endless torture; while the sweat
> Of their great agony, wrung out from this
> Their Phlegethon, curls round the rocks of jet
> That guard the gulf around, in pitiless horror set.

It is at once obvious that variation in metrical stress is combined with a preponderance of 's' sounds, both voiced and unvoiced, to reinforce powerfully the sense of the passage, the description of a waterfall, with the sound. It will hardly be necessary to note all the variations of rhythmic stress. We need refer only to those of special significance in relation to the general effect. For example, the second half of the first line. In the third foot there is only the lightest of stresses. In the next two feet three syllables out of four are stressed, two strongly, one fairly strongly. That suggests, by the massing of stresses, the take-off of the weight of water. In line four the onomatopoeic effect of the voiced and unvoiced 's' sounds is strongly reinforced by the three successive strong stresses in the middle of the line. Similarly, in line seven the impression of the boiling mass of water at the base of the fall is intensified by the first two feet, iambus and spondee, balanced by the spondee in the fourth foot.

3. Read carefully through the following passage from the fifth stanza of Tennyson's *Lotos-Eaters*:

How sweet it were, hearing the downward stream,
With half-shut eyes ever to seem
Falling asleep in a half-dream!
To dream and dream, like yonder amber light,
Which will not leave the myrrh-bush on the height;
To hear each other's whispered speech;
Eating the Lotos day by day,
To watch the crisping ripples on the beach,
    And tender curving lines of creamy spray;
To lend our hearts and spirits wholly
To the influence of mild-minded melancholy;
To muse and brood and live again in memory,
With those old faces of our infancy
Heap'd over with a mound of grass,
Two handfuls of white dust, shut in an urn of brass!

In the first line, after the first two feet, which are both iambic, the inverted stress of the next syllable strikes one of the key-notes of the passage, introducing in the syllable *hear* the vowel sound (already heard in the word *sweet*) of the word 'dream', which is to act as an undertone throughout the whole passage. It actually occurs no fewer than fifteen times in the whole passage, and all in stressed syllables. As if to underline this point, the third line begins with an inverted stress, and in the second foot reverts to the iambus, the stressed syllable being (a)*sleep*, which contains the dominant vowel sound. Another undertone in the passage is the frequent reinforcement by initial, medial, and terminal 'm's' of the soporific murmur of the passage. A trailing alexandrine, with the slowing effect of three successive stressed syllables, in the middle of the line, completes the sound pattern. Another point to notice is the alliteration and assonance in the two gently moving iambic lines in the middle of the passage.

> To watch the crisping ripples on the beach,
> And tender curving lines of creamy spray.

4. Modern poets experiment greatly with metre, often in such a way as to suggest that regular orthodox poetic rhythms are to be avoided, and that they deliberately choose rhythms more akin to those of prose. Often, as in the poem below, the apparent irregularity has a purpose, and produces a decidedly striking and pleasing effect.

> After the first powerful plain manifesto
> The black statement of pistons, without more fuss
> But gliding like a queen, she leaves the station.
> Without bowing and with restrained unconcern
> She passes the houses which humbly crowd outside,
> The gasworks and at last the heavy page
> Of death, printed by gravestones in the cemetery.
> Beyond the town there lies the open country
> Where, gathering speed, she acquires mystery,
> The luminous self-possession of ships on ocean.
> It is now she begins to sing—at first quite low
> Then loud, and at last with a jazzy madness—
> The song of her whistle screaming at curves,
> Of deafening tunnels, brakes, innumerable bolts.
> And always light, aerial, underneath
> Goes the elate metre of her wheels.
> Steaming through metal landscape on her lines
> She plunges new eras of wild happiness
> Where speed throws up strange shapes, broad curves

And parallels clean like the steel of guns.
At last, further than Edinburgh or Rome,
Beyond the crest of the world, she reaches night
Where only a low streamline brightness
Of phosphorus on the tossing hills is white.
Ah, like a comet through flame she moves entranced
Wrapt in her music no bird song, no, nor bough
Breaking with honey buds, shall ever equal.

STEPHEN SPENDER: *The Express*

The first point to notice about this poem is that its metre does not appear to correspond closely to any orthodox rhythmic system, iambic, trochaic, anapaestic, dactylic, or any combination that we are accustomed to meet. It does, however, suggest, by its system of stresses, the rhythmic movement of a railway train, starting from a station, gathering speed, and travelling on with all the variations of streaming motion, jolts, and bumps which make up the rhythmic record of a railway journey. The poet will certainly have his own views on the way to scan his poem. They may be different from ours or yours, but that is no reason why we should not make our own attempt, merely in order to suggest how the rhythmic movement of the poem appears to us.

The second point is that, if we attempt to scan the poem in the usual way, it is, without undue straining, divisible into metric feet, with rather more inverted stresses and spondees than we have learnt to deal with in scanning poetry, with an occasional intrusive dactyl or anapaest.

The third point is that when all allowance has been made for feminine endings, initial and medial hypermetric syllables, and possible elisions, the lines are not normal decasyllabics. Some of the lines have eleven, some twelve syllables, a few have ten. One line, with a great preponderance of stressed syllables, has only eight.

The following metrical analysis of the first seven lines is tentative. It seems to the writer to indicate where the strong stresses should occur if the poem is to be read conveniently, and is to suggest the actual sound of a train moving out of a station, and gradually gathering speed. The division into feet is also tentative, and is intended for comparison with poems of more regular, or conventionally regular, rhythmic pattern. Copy out the lines from the printed poem, and try for yourself. See wherein you agree and wherein you differ. It will be a useful exercise for you.

Àfter the | fìrst pòwer|ful plàin | máni|festò
The blàck | statèment of | pìstons, | withoùt | morè fùss
But glìd|ing líke | a queèn, | she leàves | the stàt(ion).
Withoùt | bowìng | ànd with res|traìned un|concèrn
She pàss|es the hoùs|es which hùm|bly crowd | outsìde,
The gàs|works and | at làst | the heàv|y pàge
Of deàth, | prìnted by | gràvestones | ín the | cemèt(e)ry.

If you try to analyse the rest of the poem you will find that departure from more regular systems of accentuation has its advantages, at least in a poem on this kind of subject.

EXERCISES

Write metrical notes on the following poems, with special reference to any departure from regular rhythms, its reason and effect.

1. Sometimes with secure delight
The upland hamlets will invite,
When the merry bells ring round,
And the jocund rebecks sound
To many a youth and many a maid,
Dancing in the chequer'd shade;
And young and old come forth to play
On a sunshine holy-day,

Till the live-long daylight fail:
Then to the spicy nut-brown ale,
With stories told of many a feat,
How Faery Mab the junkets eat.

JOHN MILTON: *L'Allegro*

2. Felix Randal the farrier, O he is dead then? my duty all ended,
Who have watched his mould of man, big-boned and hardy-handsome
Pining, pining, till time when reason rambled in it and some
Fatal four disorders, fleshed there, all contended?

Sickness broke him. Impatient he cursed at first, but mended
Being anointed and all; though a heavenlier heart began some
Months earlier, since I had our sweet reprieve and ransom
Tendered to him. Ah well, God rest him all road ever he offended!

GERARD MANLEY HOPKINS: *Felix Randal*

3. But the other swiftly strode from ridge to ridge,
Clothed with his breath, and looking as he walk'd,
Larger than human on the frozen hills.
He heard the deep behind him, and a cry
Before. His own thought drove him like a goad.
Dry clash'd his harness in the icy caves
And barren chasms, and all to left and right
The bare black cliff clang'd round him, as he based
His feet on juts of slippery crag that rang
Sharp-smitten with the dint of armed heels—
And on a sudden, lo! the level lake,
And the long glories of the winter moon.

LORD TENNYSON: *The Passing of Arthur*

4. Calme was the day, and through the trembling ayre
Sweet-breathing Zephyrus did softly play
A gentle spirit, that lightly did delay
Hot Titans beames, which then did glyster fayre;
When I, (whom sullein care,
Through discontent of my long fruitless stay
In Princes Court, and expectation vayne
Of idle hopes, which still doe fly away,
Like empty shaddowes, did afflict my brayne,)
Walkt forth to ease my payne
Along the shore of silver streaming Themmes;
Whose rutty Bancke, he which his River hemmes

Was paynted all with variable flowers,
And all the meades adornd with daintie gemmes
Fit to deck maydens bowres,
And crowne their Paramours
Against the Brydale day, which is not long:
Sweete Themmes! runne softly, till I end my Song.

EDMUND SPENSER: *Prothalamion*

5. Thou takest up
Thou know'st not what; but take it for thy labour:
It is a thing I made, which hath the king
Five times redeem'd from death: I do not know
What is more cordial: nay, I prithee, take it;
It is an earnest of a further good
That I mean to thee. Tell thy mistress how
The case stands with her; do't as from thyself.
Think what a chance thou changest on; but think
Thou hast thy mistress still, to boot, my son,
Who shall take notice of thee: I'll move the king
To any shape of thy preferment, such
As thou'lt desire; and then myself, I chiefly,
That set thee on to this desert, am bound
To load thy merit richly. Call my women:
Think on my words.

WILLIAM SHAKESPEARE: *Cymbeline*

6. At the round earth's imagined corners, blow
Your trumpets, Angels, and arise, arise
From death, you numberless infinities
Of souls, and to your scattered bodies go:
All whom the flood did, and fire shall overthrow,
All whom war, dearth, age, agues, tyrannies,
Despair, law, chance hath slain, and you whose eyes
Shall behold God, and never taste death's woe:
But let them sleep, Lord, and me mourn a space,
For, if above all these my sins abound,
'Tis late to ask abundance of Thy grace,
When we are there. Here on this lowly ground
Teach me how to repent; for that's as good
As if Thou had'st sealed my pardon with Thy blood.

JOHN DONNE: *Resurrection*

7. There is the moral of all human tales;
'Tis but the same rehearsal of the past,
First Freedom, and then Glory—when that fails,
Wealth, vice, corruption,—barbarism at last.
And History, with all her volumes vast,
Hath but one page,—'tis better written here
Where gorgeous Tyranny hath thus amass'd
All treasures, all delights, that eye or ear,
Heart, soul could seek, tongue ask—Away with words! draw near.

LORD BYRON: *Childe Harold's Pilgrimage*

8. *AGAINST ANGER*

The boy asking—in a swing travelling to the moon
through curled ice of the spinney frozen with flowers—
'The bery old man in the moon, does he wear a beret?'
The poet in the glassy office doorway,
unable to remember the Professor's Christian name;
and the man I love, in another glass
seeing his looks of delight as an unlikeable face
and his eloquence as a hum, surprised at our prizing,
had such humility I think they cannot be wounded,
their unmeant sweetness makes them a safe place.
Next when I kill them in my heart for harms
I think they do me, and when next am raging,
this remembering, let it save
my mind from the hell-go-round of the grievance-ridden,
save the fool turkeycock into love.

ANNE RIDLER: *Against Anger*

9. We that are of purer fire,
Imitate the starry quire,
Who, in their nightly watchful spheres,
Lead in swift round the months and years,
The sounds and seas, with all their finny drove,
Now to the moon in wavering morrice move;
And on the tawny sands and shelves
Trip the pert faeries and the dapper elves.

JOHN MILTON: *Comus*

10. The night is chill; the forest bare;
Is it the wind that moaneth bleak?
There is not wind enough in the air
To move away the ringlet curl
From the lovely lady's cheek—

There is not wind enough to twirl
The one red leaf, the last of its clan,
That dances as often as dance it can,
Hanging so light and hanging so high,
On the topmost twig that looks up at the sky.

Hush, beating heart of Christabel!
Jesu, Maria, shield her well!
She folded her arms beneath her cloak,
And stole to the other side of the oak.
What sees she there?

S. T. COLERIDGE: *Christabel*

11. 'Tis dead night round about: horror doth creep
And move on with the shades; stars nod, and sleep,
And through the dark air spin a fiery thread
Such as doth gild the lazy glow-worm's bed.
Yet burn'st thou there, a full day, while I spend
My rest in cares, and to the dark world lend
These flames, as thou dost thine to me; I watch
That hour, which must thy life and mine despatch;
But still thou dost outgo me, I can see
Met in thy flames all acts of piety;
Thy light is charity; thy heat is zeal;
And thy aspiring, active fires reveal
Devotion still on wing: then, thou dost weep
Still as thou burn'st, and the warm droppings creep
To measure out thy length, as if thou'dst know
What stock, and how much time were left thee now.

HENRY VAUGHAN: *The Lamp*

12. They but now who seem'd
In bigness to surpass earth's giant sons,
Now less than smallest dwarfs, in narrow room
Throng numberless, like that pygmean race

Beyond the Indian mount, or faery elves,
Whose midnight revels, by a forest-side
Or fountain, some belated peasant sees,
Or dreams he sees, while over head the moon
Sits arbitress, and nearer to the earth
Wheels her pale course; they on their mirth and dance
Intent, with jocund music charm his ear;
At once with joy and fear his heart rebounds.

JOHN MILTON: *Paradise Lost*

13. Nay, some I hav seen wil choose a beehive for their sign
and gloss their soul-delusion with a muddled thought,
picturing a skep of straw, the beekeeper's device,
a millowner's workshop, for totem of their tribe;
Not knowing the high goal of our great endeavour
is spiritual attainment, individual worth,
at all cost to be sought and at all cost pursued,
to be won at all cost and at all cost assured;
not such material ease as might be attain'd for all
by cheap production and distribution of common needs,
wer all life level'd down to where the lowest can reach:

ROBERT BRIDGES: *The Testament of Beauty*, Bk. II

14. Down in the valley not a bird-note calls,
and on the barren mountain-top only
the harsh voice of the wind speaks in the dark:
the lamentable wind through the thin grasses
blowing, and crying round the lonely rocks.
But in this hollow, on the highest ridge,
comes through the darkness the perpetual lap
of little herded companies of waves
on the rough shingle—the whispering of those
who crowd together waiting. Not a lamp
in village or on road; the earth's deep bulk
invisible; in the sky nor moon nor star:
black night—and through the night only the sounds
of wind and little waves that wait the dawn.

J. REDWOOD ANDERSON: *The Tarn*

CHAPTER VII

TRYING IT OUT

I

THIS chapter is not intended to give you a complete critical method, a sure and safe approach to all the problems with which you may have to deal, but rather to afford you a little practice in looking at poetry from various angles, so that you may get into the habit of considering any poem you are studying from as many different points of view as possible, and gradually build up a critical method of your own.

Let us begin by comparing three poems on similar themes, Robert Herrick's *To Daffodils*, William Wordsworth's *The Daffodils*, and Robert Bridges's *Cheddar Pinks*, in the light of two definitions of poetry:

A. 'Poetry is at bottom a criticism of life.'

MATTHEW ARNOLD

B. 'Primarily poetry is an exploration of the possibilities of language.' MICHAEL ROBERTS

THREE POEMS

1. *TO DAFFODILS*

Fair Daffodils, we weep to see
  You haste away so soon:
As yet the early-rising Sun
  Has not attain'd his noon.
    Stay, stay,
  Until the hasting day
    Has run
  But to the even-song;
And, having pray'd together, we
  Will go with you along.

We have short time to stay, as you,
  We have as short a Spring;
As quick a growth to meet decay
  As you, or any thing.
    We die,
  As your hours do, and dry
    Away
  Like to the Summer's rain;
Or as the pearls of morning's dew,
  Ne'er to be found again.

ROBERT HERRICK

2. *THE DAFFODILS*

I wandered lonely as a cloud
  That floats on high o'er vales and hills,
When all at once I saw a crowd,
  A host, of golden daffodils,
Beside the lake, beneath the trees,
Fluttering and dancing in the breeze.

Continuous as the stars that shine
  And twinkle on the milky way,
They stretched in never-ending line
  Along the margin of a bay:
Ten thousand saw I at a glance
Tossing their heads in sprightly dance.

The waves beside them danced, but they
  Out-did the sparkling waves in glee:
A Poet could not but be gay
  In such a jocund company!
I gazed—and gazed—but little thought
What wealth the show to me had brought:

For oft, when on my couch I lie
  In vacant or in pensive mood,
They flash upon that inward eye
  Which is the bliss of solitude;
And then my heart with pleasure fills,
And dances with the daffodils.

WILLIAM WORDSWORTH

3. *CHEDDAR PINKS*

Mid the squander'd colour
  idling as I lay
Reading the Odyssey
  in my rock-garden
I espied the cluster'd
  tufts of Cheddar pinks
Burgeoning with promise
  of their scented bloom
All the modish motley
  of their bloom to-be
Thrust up in narrow buds
  on the slender stalks
Thronging springing urgent
  hasting (so I thought)
As if they feared to be
  too late for summer—
Like schoolgirls overslept
  waken'd by the bell
Leaping from bed to don
  their muslin dresses
    On a May morning:
Then felt I like to one
  indulging in sin
(Whereto Nature is oft
  a blind accomplice)

Because my aged bones
  so enjoyed the sun
There as I lay along
  idling with my thoughts
Reading an old poet
  while the busy world
Toil'd moil'd fuss'd and scurried
  worried bought and sold
Plotted stole and quarrel'd
  fought and God knows what.
I had forgotten Homer
  dallying with my thoughts
Till I fell to making
  these little verses
Communing with the flowers
  in my rock-garden
    on a May morning.

ROBERT BRIDGES

A. 1. The criticism of, or judgement on, life that is suggested by Herrick's poem is that all things, animate or inanimate, are transient,

We have *short* time to *stay*, as you,
We have as *short* a Spring.

That idea induces a mood of sadness.

we *weep* to see
You haste away so soon:

Finally, the poet in the last lines implies that, as with the daffodils, so with human beings, this life is all.

The quick, occasionally staccato rhythm suggests that the mood may be just a passing whim of the poet. There is no actual description of the flowers, no attempt to suggest anything about them except their transience. The poet does not even mention their beauty, except by the single epithet 'fair'.

2. Wordsworth seems, at first sight, mainly concerned with the daffodils for their own sake. If there is any criticism of, or judgement on, life, it would appear to be a sense of joy in the fact that natural beauty is a part of our environment. He describes the colour of the daffodils, the way they grow in clusters, their sprightly movements in the breeze, their gaiety, their twinkling brightness. Towards the end of the third stanza, however, a reflective element appears, to be developed in the last stanza. The daffodils serve to communicate a sense of joy to the poet, almost as though they were the voice of God suggesting, not the transience and mortality of all earthly things, but the joy and beauty to be found in life.

3. *Cheddar Pinks* differs from the other poems in that the pinks suggest the active world, outside both the poet and the pinks themselves.

For Herrick the daffodils symbolize transience.

For Wordsworth they symbolize beauty and gaiety.

For Bridges the Cheddar Pinks symbolize the bustle and toil of the outer world.

Yet though the pinks by their activity, their thronging, springing, urgent character, seem to reproach the poet for his idleness, nature, of which they are a part, is his accomplice.

As in Wordsworth's *Daffodils*, the reflective element in *Cheddar Pinks* does not serve to communicate a sense of frustration, and of the transience of life. Rather it suggests the stir and movement of a striving world.

B. Exploration of the possibilities of language:

1. What is the dominating idea in the 'word-pattern' of the poem *To Daffodils*?

The pattern is dominated by the idea of the swift transience of things natural and mortal.

Haste—hasting—has run.
Short time—as short a spring.
Quick a growth to meet decay.
We die—and dry away.
Ne'er to be found again.

The ideas of haste and transience are further reinforced by the alternation of short and very short lines.

2. In Wordsworth's *The Daffodils* the word-pattern is more complex. Several different ideas are suggested:

Colour.	Golden. Though this word is used only once, it helps greatly to evoke the appropriate picture.
Multitude.	Crowd—host—ten thousand.
Movement.	Fluttering, dancing, sprightly dance (contrast with the first two lines of stanza one).
Gaiety.	Dancing—tossing their heads—jocund.
Brightness.	(Compared with stars) twinkle—(compared with waves) sparkling—flash.

Note the sober tints in the last stanza:

Vacant, pensive, inward eye, bliss of solitude (compared with *jocund*).

These sober tints are harmonized with the general pattern of the last stanza, the last line of which re-introduces the gayer trend of the first three stanzas.

3. In *Cheddar Pinks* the word-pattern is not one of interwoven strands as in *The Daffodils*. It is a poem in 'couple-colour'.

1. The Pinks—their *squander'd* colour (clustered tufts, modish motley), their scented bloom, narrow buds, slender stalks—thrusting, springing, urgent.

Note the emotive force of the single word *squander'd*. It suggests as much as is suggested by many words—crowd, host, ten thousand, company—in Wordsworth's poem.

Note, too, the balance of the phrases, *burgeoning with promise . . . their bloom to-be*.

Note the aptness of the simile of the school-girls. There are two points of comparison:

(i) The urgency of the pinks—thronging—springing—urgent—hasting.

The urgency of the schoolgirls—overslept—leaping from bed.

(ii) The lightness of the pinks—narrow buds—slender stalks.

The lightness of the girls—muslin dresses.

2. The idleness of the poet—aged bones—lay along—idling, dallying with my thoughts.

The business of the world—Toiled, moiled, fussed, scurried, worried, bought, sold. . . .

2

Let us now examine two poems in the light of another saying of Matthew Arnold, very similar to the one quoted in the early part of this chapter, but with a little more detail.

'The grand power of poetry is its interpretative power, the power of so dealing with things as to awaken in us a wonderfully new and intimate sense of them, and of our relations with them.'

1. *THE QUIET LIFE*

Happy the man, whose wish and care
A few paternal acres bound,
Content to breathe his native air
In his own ground.

Whose herds with milk, whose fields with bread,
  Whose flocks supply him with attire;
Whose trees in summer yield him shade,
    In winter fire.

Blest, who can unconcern'dly find
  Hours, days, and years slide soft away
In health of body, peace of mind,
    Quiet by day,

Sound sleep by night; study and ease
  Together mix'd; sweet recreation,
And innocence, which most does please
    With meditation.

Thus let me live, unseen, unknown;
  Thus unlamented let me die;
Steal from the world, and not a stone
    Tell where I lie.

ALEXANDER POPE

What does the poem interpret for us? It fuses in a new setting the old Horatian virtue of self-sufficiency and moderation, the Christian virtue of acceptance and resignation, and the Victorian ideal of contentment in the station in life to which God has called us. The true blessings of life, argues the poet, are the commonplace and ordinary things to which we are heirs, in which we should be wise to live and die—a few paternal acres, native air, bread, simple clothing, health, peace, quietude, sleep, innocence, and inconspicuousness.

Note the following significant words and phrases, which bear the weight of the poem:

Happy . . . few
Unconcern'dly
Slide soft away
Unseen . . . unknown
Steal . . . not a stone.

2. *EVE*

Eve, with her basket, was
Deep in the bells and grass,
Wading in bells and grass
Up to her knees,
Picking a dish of sweet
Berries and plums to eat,
Down in the bells and grass
Under the trees.

Mute as a mouse in a
Corner the cobra lay,
Curled round a bough of the
Cinnamon tall . . .
Now to get even and
Humble proud heaven and
Now was the moment or
Never at all.

'Eva!' Each syllable
Light as a flower fell,
'Eva!' he whispered the
Wondering maid,
Soft as a bubble sung
Out of a linnet's lung,
Soft and most silverly
'Eva!' he said.

Picture that orchard sprite,
Eve, with her body white,
Supple and smooth to her
Slim finger tips,

Wondering, listening,
Listening, wondering,
Eve with a berry
Half-way to her lips.

Oh had our simple Eve
Seen through the make-believe!
Had she but known the
Pretender he was!
Out of the boughs he came,
Whispering still her name,
Tumbling in twenty rings
Into the grass.

Here was the strangest pair
In the world anywhere,
Eve in the bells and grass
Kneeling, and he
Telling his story low . . .
Singing birds saw them go
Down the dark path to
The Blasphemous Tree.

Oh what a clatter when
Titmouse and Jenny Wren
Saw him successful and
Taking his leave!
How the birds rated him,
How they all hated him!
How they all pitied
Poor motherless Eve!

Picture her crying
Outside in the lane,
Eve, with no dish of sweet
Berries and plums to eat,

Haunting the gate of the
Orchard in vain . . .
Picture the lewd delight
Under the hill to-night—
'Eva!' the toast goes round,
'Eva!' again.

RALPH HODGSON

PRELIMINARIES

1. Tell the story of Adam and Eve, their temptation and expulsion from the Garden of Eden.

2. What ideas have you formed in your mind of Adam and Eve respectively?

Now turn to the poem.

1. What impression of Eve do you get from the poem? She seems almost a child, a simple, sweet child.

2. What impression do you get of Satan? Simply that of some insidious creature trying to get even with its enemy, and then undergoing various changes.

3. In the third stanza Satan seems a slim, silver-tongued, seductive youth.

4. In the fourth stanza we get a vital impression of Eve as a very young, simple, wistful, wondering child.

5. In the sixth stanza the distance between the pair seems to have lengthened. Eve is still a child, though now a half-defeated child. Satan seems older, having established an ascendancy, though there is nothing very definite to go on, except Eve's attention, his grave low tones, and her following him.

6. This impression is intensified in the seventh stanza, by the evidence of the chattering, scandalized creatures of nature.

7. In the last stanza Eve is still a child, though a tearful child, less a sinner than a forlorn, tricked child, bereft of the bright glory of life. Satan has now become the loose man of the world, who boasts of his conquests with his evil companions.

QUESTION

Does not this poem interpret for us an old story, that of the fall of man, making it seem nearer, and more interesting, vital, and fresh? Again, do we not feel that here is a drama with which we are every day familiar, another version of the age-old struggle between good and evil in the world?

Note the emotive words:

Deep — wading — Mute — bubble — linnet's lung — silverly—sprite . . . white—supple . . . smooth—slim—half-way to her lips—Blasphemous—crying—haunting—lewd—toast.

3

A. 'All good poetry is the spontaneous overflow of powerful feelings.' WILLIAM WORDSWORTH

B. 'Primarily poetry is an exploration of the possibilities of language.' MICHAEL ROBERTS

TWO POEMS

1. *SONG OF THE EMIGRANTS IN BERMUDA*

Where the remote Bermudas ride
In the ocean's bosom unespied,
From a small boat that row'd along
The listening winds received this song:
'What should we do but sing His praise
That led us through the watery maze
Unto an isle so long unknown,
And yet far kinder than our own?
Where He the huge sea-monsters wracks,
That lift the deep upon their backs,
He lands us on a grassy stage,
Safe from the storm and prelate's rage:

He gave us this eternal spring
Which here enamels everything,
And sends the fowls to us in care
On daily visits through the air;
He hangs in shades the orange bright
Like golden lamps in a green night,
And does in the pomegranates close
Jewels more rich than Ormus shows:
He makes the figs our mouths to meet,
And throws the melons at our feet;
But apples plants of such a price,
No tree could ever bear them twice.
With cedars chosen by His hand
From Lebanon He stores the land;
And makes the hollow seas that roar
Proclaim the ambergris on shore.
He cast (of which we rather boast)
The Gospel's pearl upon our coast;
And in these rocks for us did frame
A temple where to sound His name.
Oh! let our voice His praise exalt
Till it arrive at Heaven's vault,
Which thence (perhaps) rebounding may
Echo beyond the Mexique bay!'
Thus sung they in the English boat
An holy and a cheerful note:
And all the way, to guide their chime
With falling oars they kept the time.

ANDREW MARVELL

2. *THE LITTLE DANCERS*

Lonely, save for a few faint stars, the sky
Dreams; and lonely, below, the little street
Into its gloom retires, secluded and shy.

Scarcely the dumb roar enters this soft retreat;
And all is dark, save where come flooding rays
From a tavern window: there, to the brisk measure
Of an organ that down in an alley merrily plays,
Two children, all alone and no one by,
Holding their tattered frocks, thro' an airy maze
Of motion lightly threaded with nimble feet
Dance sedately; face to face they gaze,
Their eyes shining, grave with a perfect pleasure.

LAURENCE BINYON

A. 1. The poem expresses an intense religious devotion, characteristic of Marvell's own age, and constantly recurrent in human experience.

It also expresses a sense of exaltation in the lavish profusion of God's gifts to man. There is almost an Hebraic conception of a land flowing with milk and honey. In fact Marvell's hyperbolic style is constantly reminiscent of the Hebraic scriptures.

2. Binyon's beautiful little poem breathes the spirit of mystery, awe, and quiet beauty which a deserted street inspires in a thoughtful mind.

It also suggests a belief in 'Animism'. The word 'dreams' implies that even the sky has a soul and sentient being. (Cf. Matthew Arnold's 'dreaming garden trees'.)

The poet seems struck by a powerful sense of the contrast between the noise of the outside world and the quiet of the street (dumb roar . . . soft retreat).

B. 1. The metaphorical use of the word 'ride' gives a peculiarly satisfying picture of a group of islands anchored peacefully like a fleet after the turmoil of the sea, and suggests also the arrival of the emigrants in their spiritual haven after the religious storms which had racked them.

Note, too, the vivid image in line 10.

Though the word 'enamels' is a somewhat conventional expression, it has a certain aptness here. It suits the pastel-like quality of the poem. So, too, does the quaintness of the expression in lines 15–16. The charming, though fanciful, simile in lines 17–18 is, too, in harmony with the spirit of the poem, as, also, is the imaginative hyperbole in lines 23–4.

It may be, perhaps, fanciful to suggest that in line 29 the poet is exploring the possibilities of anti-climax to produce a quaintness in humorous effect!

2. One little miracle this poem accomplishes is the harmonizing of contrasted ideas, to produce a perfect fusion. This is seen in the contrast between the sleeping street and the dancing children, and between the sedate gravity of the children and their gaiety, and the way the poet handles the contrasts.

Another happy effect is the succession of quaint and lovely parallels:

The *lonely* sky . . . the children all *alone*.

The sky *dreams* . . . the *shy* little streets (suggestive of a soul in inanimate things).

The *tattered* frocks (normally suggestive of drab misery, but transformed by the whole tenour of the poem) . . . the beauty of the *ugly* streets.

Another highly emotive suggestion is that of the shining-eyed children threading an airy maze of motion.

Note the word-pattern, many strands being woven into a beautiful unity. Words suggesting:

1. *Loneliness.*	Lonely, few, secluded, alone, no one by.
2. *Darkness.*	Faint, gloom, dark.
3. *Light.*	Flooding rays.
4. *Life of the inanimate.*	Dreams, shy.
5. *Quietude.*	Dreams, shy, sedately.

6. *Noise.* Roar, plays.
7. *Human life.* Tavern-window, two children, dance, face to face, eyes shining.
8. *Sordidness.* Tattered.
9. *Grace.* Airy, lightly, nimble.
10. *Serenity.* Sedately, grave with perfect pleasure.
11. *Joy.* Pleasure, merrily, eyes shining.

NOTE. These, and any other poems, may be considered in the light of any other of the 'starting-points' mentioned in Chapter I. It will be a useful exercise for you to judge poems from as many points of view as possible.

4

Though *every* work of art should have unity of idea, some general conception or central theme, pervading the whole, some forms of poetry seem particularly dependent for their full effect upon such unity. Unity of idea is an essential characteristic of a good sonnet. Sometimes the theme may be expressed in general terms in the sonnet, sometimes the idea may be found in the first eight lines, the last six containing a particular application of it. Consider the following sonnets, the first by Shakespeare, the second by Wordsworth. Shakespeare's is, of course, written in his own loose rhyming structure; it is virtually three quatrains, alternately rhyming, rounded off by a rhyming couplet. Wordsworth's is on the 'Guittonian' model, that which Petrarch adopted in his sonnets.

1. *TRUE LOVE*

Let me not to the marriage of true minds
    Admit impediments. Love is not love
Which alters when it alteration finds,
    Or bends with the remover to remove:—

O no! it is an ever-fixed mark
  That looks on tempests, and is never shaken;
It is the star to every wandering bark,
  Whose worth 's unknown, although his height be taken.

Love 's not Time's fool, though rosy lips and cheeks
  Within his bending sickle's compass come;
Love alters not with his brief hours and weeks,
  But bears it out ev'n to the edge of doom:—

If this be error, and upon me proved,
I never writ, nor no man ever loved.

WILLIAM SHAKESPEARE

2. *UPON WESTMINSTER BRIDGE*

Earth has not anything to show more fair:
  Dull would he be of soul who could pass by
    A sight so touching in its majesty:
  This City now doth like a garment wear

  The beauty of the morning: silent, bare,
    Ships, towers, domes, theatres, and temples lie
    Open unto the fields, and to the sky,
  All bright and glittering in the smokeless air.

  Never did sun more beautifully steep
    In his first splendour valley, rock, or hill;
  Ne'er saw I, never felt, a calm so deep!

    The river glideth at his own sweet will:
  Dear God! the very houses seem asleep;
    And all that mighty heart is lying still!

WILLIAM WORDSWORTH

1. The theme of Shakespeare's sonnet is the idea that true love is unchanged by time or circumstance.

In the first quatrain he states the theme.

In the second he expresses metaphorically the idea contained in the last line of the first quatrain, the steadfastness of true love. Love is an ever-fixed mark, a star to the mariner.

Unlike mortals, love does not fall to the sickle of Time.

The concluding couplet merely states in general terms the unassailable truth of the proposition.

2. In Wordsworth's sonnet the unity is one not so much of theme as of atmosphere; it is a descriptive unity, the serene beauty of London in the early morning.

In the first eight lines this beauty is described in general terms: in the last six one particular aspect of that beauty is treated, the calm of the city steeped in the first rays of the morning sun.

Notes on the Language of the Poems

1. The poem opens with an allusion to the marriage banns. No one can forbid the banns of true love. There are no lawful *impediments*. True love cannot be *altered*, does not *bend* to force. Love stands like a sea-mark. (Note. Shakespeare uses this simile in *Coriolanus*, as a symbol for steadfastness—'and stick i' the wars Like a great sea-mark, standing every flaw'.) Love is as fixed as the Pole Star that guides the mariner.

Many will find the metaphor in lines 7–8 most telling if left unexplained, suggesting the limitless power of true love. Broadly speaking, it may mean that just as the influence of the stars in the stellar system is unknown—at least in Shakespeare's time—although astrologers have determined its altitude by means of the astrolabe, so the full strength of love is incalculable, though certain of its eternal manifestations are measurable.

It is impossible to over-estimate the concrete emotive significance of the conventional word 'rosy' in line 9. In the context it is a vital epithet, colouring the abstractions of the sonnet with the warm flush of vigorous life. The physical body of the lover may be the sport of Time, true love can never be.

2. A good deal of the beauty of this poem lies in its rhythmic undertones, the smooth flow of the lines suggesting the river passing beneath the bridge in the calm of the early morning. Though the undertones are felt throughout the poem, they are particularly marked in the sestet. Other points to be noted are:

1. The full emotive force of the phrase 'like a garment'. It suggests not only that its beauty is something the city assumes in the early morning, but that it is a beauty which clings to the city, enveloping it like a fine fabric, a dawn veil of infinite and delicate loveliness. The phrase gives a vital picture of the rose-suffused mists gradually melting away, to reveal for a moment the significant detail of the city, at its zenith of magical charm.
2. The word 'steep', which suggests a London bathed in and impregnated with a rich filmy sunlight, which brightens as the mists die away.
3. The beauty of line 12, which is largely a rhythmic beauty, and seems to depend on the word 'glideth', suggesting, as it does, a quiet and sinuous movement in keeping with the spirit of the poem, and with such words and phrases as 'silent', 'a calm so deep', 'is lying still'.

5

It is one of the commonplaces of criticism that Shakespeare's blank verse progressed from formal regularity in his earlier plays to extreme freedom of movement in his later ones. It is useful, at times, to analyse differences between the earlier and later styles. Such an exercise may teach you something of the dates of Shakespeare's plays, and a good deal that is more useful of Shakespeare's poetic style. What is more valuable still, it will give you some insight into the way a great poet handles the ideas which are the very stuff of which his poetry is made.

Let us compare, or rather contrast, the two passages from Shakespeare's plays, the first from *Love's Labour's Lost*, the second from *Hamlet*.

1. *Biron.* This fellow pecks up wit as pigeons pease,
And utters it again when God doth please:
He is wit's pedler, and retails his wares
At wakes and wassails, meetings, markets, fairs;
And we that sell by gross, the Lord doth know,
Have not the grace to grace it with such show.
This gallant pins the wenches on his sleeve;
Had he been Adam, he had tempted Eve;
A' can carve too, and lisp; why, this is he
That kiss'd his hand away in courtesy;
This is the ape of form, monsieur the nice,
That, when he plays at tables, chides the dice
In honourable terms: nay, he can sing
A mean most meanly; and in ushering,
Mend him who can: the ladies call him sweet;
The stairs, as he treads on them, kiss his feet:
This is the flower that smiles on every one,
To show his teeth as white as whale's bone;
And consciences, that will not die in debt,
Pay him the due of honey-tongued Boyet.

Love's Labour's Lost

2. *Hamlet.* To be, or not to be: that is the question:
Whether 'tis nobler in the mind to suffer
The slings and arrows of outrageous fortune,
Or to take arms against a sea of troubles,
And by opposing end them. To die; to sleep;

No more; and by a sleep to say we end
The heart-ache, and the thousand natural shocks
That flesh is heir to, 'tis a consummation
Devoutly to be wish'd. To die, to sleep;
To sleep: perchance to dream: ay there 's the rub;
For in that sleep of death what dreams may come,
When we have shuffled off this mortal coil,
Must give us pause: there 's the respect
That makes calamity of so long life;
For who would bear the whips and scorns of time,
The oppressor's wrong, the proud man's contumely,
The pangs of despised love, the law's delay,
The insolence of office, and the spurns
That patient merit of the unworthy takes,
When he himself might his quietus make
With a bare bodkin? who would fardels bear,
To grunt and sweat under a weary life,
But that the dread of something after death,
The undiscover'd country from whose bourn
No traveller returns, puzzles the will,
And makes us rather bear those ills we have
Than fly to others that we know not of?
Thus conscience does make cowards of us all,
And thus the native hue of resolution
Is sicklied o'er with the pale cast of thought,
And enterprises of great pitch and moment
With this regard their currents turn awry
And lose the name of action.

Hamlet

Both these passages have a conversational ring, the first being in fact spoken to, or perhaps at, the King, the second being of that species of communing with one's listening self which is called a soliloquy. But here the comparison ends.

Biron's speech has an air of flippant, sub-acid chatter, the talk of a gay, somewhat irresponsible young man, aware of his own wit, and desirous of impressing his listener, who is also his King. It is consciously 'clever', as witness the clipped and balanced lines, and smart little metaphors. The rhyme, of course, greatly assists in the producing of this effect.

The second speech is a kind of brooding self-questioning, the spiritual racking of one deep 'cut to the brains'. We can imagine such a man speaking thus in his privacy, the voice falling now into a slow measured tone, hesitating, as the mind gropes forward, now rising and quickening, as the intolerable evils of life huddle upon him, now dying away to a slow, mournful whisper as the

> dread of something after death,
> The undiscover'd country from whose bourn
> No traveller returns

slakes the flames of his anger, and palsies his resolution.

The differences are due, partly to the nature of the respective plays, *Love's Labour's Lost* being a comedy, *Hamlet* a tragedy, partly to easily analysable technical differences, but mostly to the maturing of the poet both in the exercise of his craft and in the depth of his experience.

Let us consider first the technical differences. The passage from *Love's Labour's Lost* is in rhyme, that from *Hamlet* in blank verse. Good blank verse is always a more natural vehicle of continuous dramatic speech than rhyme. In rhyme, the sense is more often confined to the distich, and the speech becomes a series of self-contained utterances, or, as in this speech, portions of wit or sententiousness. It is language dressed for show. There are no run-on lines in this passage, except within the distich, none of the so-called irregularities which Shakespeare later permitted himself, no hypermetric syllables, no feminine endings, no weak or light endings, very little variation in the position of the medial pause. All this tends to give the speech, facile and witty as it is, an air of formality.

The metaphorical language, too, is fanciful, rather than penetrating, amusing rather than deeply disturbing or exciting. 'This fellow pecks up wit as pigeons pease,' 'This gallant pins the wenches on his sleeve,' 'This is the flower that smiles on every one.'

At times it is gracefully hyperbolic:

> this is he
> That kissed his hand away in courtesy.

Lightness of metre, imagery, and language is the prevailing characteristic.

The passage from *Hamlet* has many run-on lines, and greater variation in the position of the medial pause. This gives it the air of a sustained piece of conversation, the sense flowing on from line to line, until the thought is elaborated and completed, rather than a series of oracular utterances. In this connexion note the way Shakespeare piles clause on clause, and phrase on phrase, to get that forward-urging movement which helps so much to achieve paragraph unity.

The metaphorical language of the passage, though not of that searching depth characteristic of some of the speeches of Shakespeare's later plays, invariably touches the reader or playgoer closer than the 'taffeta phrases' of Biron's speech. The phrases of Hamlet's speech all jar some aching nerve or other: 'The slings and arrows of outrageous fortune', 'the . . . shocks that flesh is heir to', 'the whips and scorns of time', 'the undiscovered country from whose bourn no traveller returns', all probe deep until we reach the most emotion-searching metaphor in the whole passage,

> And thus the native hue of resolution
> Is sicklied o'er with the pale cast of thought.

6

'I would say that the poet may write about anything providing that that thing matters to him to start with, for then it will bring with it into the poem the intellectual or moral significance which it has for him in life.'

LOUIS MACNEICE

Two poems, *For The Fallen* by Laurence Binyon, *Mental Cases* by Wilfred Owen, are quite obviously written on something that matters to the two poets. That something equally obviously brings with it into the poems the intellectual or moral significance which it has for the poets in life. A study of the poems, however, will reveal how widely different is the significance of a similar experience to the two poets. Each poet speaks of the fallen in war, Binyon of those who have died physically, Owen of those who have died mentally.

1. *FOR THE FALLEN*

With proud thanksgiving, a mother for her children,
England mourns for her dead across the sea,
Flesh of her flesh they were, spirit of her spirit,
Fallen in the cause of the free.

Solemn the drums thrill: Death august and royal
Sings sorrow up into immortal spheres,
There is music in the midst of desolation
And a glory that shines upon our tears.

They went with songs to the battle, they were young,
Straight of limb, true of eye, steady and aglow.
They were staunch to the end against odds uncounted,
They fell with their faces to the foe.

They shall grow not old, as we that are left grow old:
Age shall not weary them, nor the years condemn.
At the going down of the sun and in the morning
We will remember them.

They mingle not with their laughing comrades again;
They sit no more at familiar tables of home;
They have no lot in our labour of the day-time:
They sleep beyond England's foam.

But where our desires are and our hopes profound,
Felt as a well-spring that is hidden from sight,
To the innermost heart of their own land they are known
As the stars are known to the Night;

As the stars that shall be bright when we are dust
Moving in marches upon the heavenly plain,
As the stars that are starry in the time of our darkness,
To the end, to the end, they remain.

LAURENCE BINYON

2. *MENTAL CASES*

Who are these? Why sit they here in twilight?
Wherefore rock they, purgatorial shadows,
Drooping tongues from jaws that slob their relish,
Baring teeth that leer like skulls' teeth wicked?
Stroke on stroke of pain,—but what slow panic,
Gouged these chasms round their fretted sockets?
Ever from their hair and through their hands' palms
Misery swelters. Surely we have perished
Sleeping, and walk hell; but who these hellish?

—These are men whose minds the Dead have ravished.
Memory fingers in their hair of murders,
Multitudinous murders they once witnessed.
Wading sloughs of flesh these helpless wander,

Treading blood from lungs that had loved laughter.
Always they must see these things and hear them,
Batter of guns and shatter of flying muscles,
Carnage incomparable, and human squander,
Rucked too thick for these men's extrication.

Therefore still their eyeballs shrink tormented
Back into their brains, because on their sense
Sunlight seems a blood-smear; night comes blood-black;
Dawn breaks open like a wound that bleeds afresh
—Thus their heads wear this hilarious, hideous,
Awful falseness of set-smiling corpses.
—Thus their hands are plucking at each other;
Picking at the rope-knouts of their scourging;
Snatching after us who smote them, brother,
Pawing us who dealt them war and madness.

WILFRED OWEN

From Binyon's poem we gather that what matter to the poet are the old heroic virtues, the love of liberty and courage, a pride in the virile inheritance of the nation, a spirit that pervades alike the early epic and ballad and the more modern heroic plays, like Shakespeare's *Henry V*. Though the tone of Binyon's poem is different it is not alien to the spirit of Henry the Fifth's Crispin speech, uttered just before the battle of Agincourt.

There is, of course, a note of mourning and a sense of bereavement throughout the poem, but deeper is that of 'proud thanksgiving', and the 'glory that shines upon our tears'.

In step with the feeling of irreparable loss marches almost triumphantly the sense that though the dead may no longer be with us in physical presence, though 'they sit no more at familiar tables of home', in all that matters most they are with us and of us, sharing our 'hopes profound', known as of old 'to the innermost heart of their own land', and journeying with us to the end.

Binyon voices here a view that many may not be disposed to echo, but he has poetized it, made it free of that poetic world which, as Lascelles Abercrombie says, 'is a world without prejudice', a world where 'the writ of those moral and practical judgements which we feel compelled to exercise does not run'.

The poem has the movement of a solemn but not sombre funeral march, the spaced accents in the short lines at the end of each stanza falling like drum taps. There is a great variety of poetic foot used, iambic, trochaic, anapaestic, dactylic, and spondaic, in keeping with the constant variation of tone. Similarly varied is the language, words expressive of the simple human affections, mother, children, laughing comrades, familiar tables, labour of the day-time, following words of high pomp and ceremonial, solemn the drums thrill, august and royal; and the words connoting bereavement, mourning, desolation, tears, are not so realistic as to clash with the spirit of the whole. The most concrete elements in the language of the poem are those of the first class. These are the most vital strands in the word-pattern, but there are other words, words, for example, expressing the sense of elevation of the human spirit, 'proud thanksgiving', 'music in the midst of desolation', 'glory that shines upon our tears', words expressing courage and virile strength, 'straight of limb', 'true of eye', 'steady and aglow', 'staunch to the end', and finally words of remembrance, 'we will remember them', 'they are known', 'they remain'.

To Wilfred Owen, what matters is not the glory of sacrifice, or the pomp of thanksgiving, or the duty of remembrance, but the mental wreckage which remains as a symbol of the intolerable indecency of war, which reduces men to a level far below that of the beasts, as it sometimes exalts them to the gods. He sees war not in abstract symbolism merely, relieved by little concrete pictures of the heroes and the familiar tables, but in a succession of vivid images of blood, spattered brains, morasses of mashed flesh, slobbering man-made imbeciles, leering distortions of God's likeness.

The mere recital of crude horrors would inevitably pall. Owen has saved his poem from this by an extremely vital use of language, and a deeply penetrating imagination.

The most telling parts of the poem are not the concrete images of horror, the shatter of flying muscles, human squander rucked thick, the leering teeth, and the set-smiling corpses, but the passages showing insight into the worst tragedy of the war's wreckage. 'These are men the Dead have *ravished*', that is, forcibly deprived of their virtue, 'memory *fingers in their hair* of murders', and greatest of all the fearful image of the hopeless dawn, 'Dawn breaks open like a wound that bleeds afresh'.

Occasionally Owen uses words in an unusual sense, with striking effect. In the second stanza, for example, he compares the plight of the mental cases to men buried inextricably beneath a pile of dead, 'human squander, Rucked too thick for these men's extrication.' By the word 'rucked', borrowing an earlier meaning, he suggests not merely the stack of bodies, but, by an association of ideas and sound, some idea of the rotting mass of human wastage.

7

Human love is one of the three great subjects which have inspired lyric poets, the other two being Death and Nature. In the following three poems, *The Good-Morrow*, by John Donne, *Sally In Our Alley*, by Henry Carey, and *Come down, O Maid*, by Lord Tennyson, the ancient theme has been treated in very different ways, owing not so much to differences of poetic technique as to a radical difference in spiritual approach.

THE GOOD-MORROW

I wonder, by my troth, what thou and I
Did, till we loved? Were we not weaned till then,
But sucked on country pleasures childishly?
Or snorted we in the seven sleepers' den?
'Twas so; but as all pleasures fancies be,
If ever any beauty I did see,
Which I desired, and got, 'twas but a dream of thee.

And now good-morrow to our waking souls,
Which watch not one another, out of fear:
For love all love of other sights controls,
And makes one little room, an everywhere.
Let sea-discoverers to new worlds have gone,
Let maps to other worlds our world have shown,
Let us possess one world, each hath one, and is one!

My face in thine eye, thine in mine appears,
And true plain hearts do in the faces rest;
Where can we find two fitter hemispheres
Without sharp North, without declining West?
Whatever dies was not mixed equally;
If our two loves be one, both thou and I
Love so alike, none of these loves can die.

JOHN DONNE

Of all the girls that are so smart
  There's none like pretty Sally;
She is the darling of my heart,
  And she lives in our alley.
There is no lady in the land
  Is half so sweet as Sally;
She is the darling of my heart,
  And she lives in our alley.

Her father he makes cabbage-nets
  And through the streets does cry 'em;
Her mother she sells laces long
  To such as please to buy 'em:
But sure such folks could ne'er beget
  So sweet a girl as Sally!
She is the darling of my heart,
  And she lives in our alley.

When she is by, I leave my work,
  I love her so sincerely;
My master comes like any Turk,
  And bangs me most severely—
But let him bang his bellyful,
  I'll bear it all for Sally;
She is the darling of my heart
  And she lives in our alley.

Of all the days that 's in the week
  I dearly love but one day—
And that 's the day that comes betwixt
  A Saturday and Monday;
For then I'm drest all in my best
  To walk abroad with Sally;
She is the darling of my heart,
  And she lives in our alley.

My master carries me to church,
  And often am I blamed
Because I leave him in the lurch
  As soon as text is named;
I leave the church in sermon-time
  And slink away to Sally;
She is the darling of my heart,
  And she lives in our alley.

When Christmas comes about again
  O then I shall have money;
I'll hoard it up, and box and all,
  I'll give it to my honey:
I would it were ten thousand pound,
  I'd give it all to Sally;
She is the darling of my heart,
  And she lives in our alley.

My master and the neighbours all
  Make game of me and Sally,
And, but for her, I'd better be
  A slave and row a galley;
But when my seven long years are out
  O then I'll marry Sally,—
O then we'll wed, and then we'll bed,
  But not in our alley!

H. CAREY

COME DOWN, O MAID . . .

Come down, O maid, from yonder mountain height:
What pleasure lives in height (the Shepherd sang),
In height and cold, the splendour of the hills?
But cease to move so near the Heavens, and cease
To glide a sunbeam by the blasted Pine,
To sit a star upon the sparkling spire;
And come, for Love is of the valley, come,
For Love is of the valley, come thou down
And find him; by the happy threshold, he,
Or hand in hand with Plenty in the maize,
Or red with spirted purple of the vats,
Or fox-like in the vine; nor cares to walk
With Death and Morning on the silver horns,
Nor wilt thou snare him in the white ravine,

Nor find him dropt upon the firths of ice,
That huddling slant in furrow-cloven falls
To roll the torrent out of dusky doors:
But follow; let the torrent dance thee down
To find him in the valley; let the wild
Lean-headed Eagles yelp alone, and leave
The monstrous ledges there to slope, and spill
Their thousand wreaths of dangling water-smoke,
That like a broken purpose waste in air:
So waste not thou; but come; for all the vales
Await thee; azure pillars of the hearth
Arise to thee; the children call, and I
Thy shepherd pipe, and sweet is every sound,
Sweeter thy voice, but every sound is sweet;
Myriads of rivulets hurrying thro' the lawn,
The moan of doves in immemorial elms,
And murmuring of innumerable bees.

LORD TENNYSON

1. Donne's poem has little of the ecstatic abandon common to many love poems, or of the amorous persiflage which the cavalier poets of his own age affected, none of the sweet verbal music characteristic of lyric poems in general, and of love poems in particular. It has many of the mannerisms to which Donne and his school are prone. It completely lacks the sentimentality and submissiveness conventional among love poets. In what Mrs. Meynell calls his 'fine onsets' it resembles some of his love poems; it lacks both the satiric twist and the macabre tinge characteristic of others. It opens magnificently:

> I wonder, by my troth, what thou and I
> Did, till we loved?

It then soon engages itself in a typical conceit, the idea that life before they loved was mere spiritual infancy, or a gross lethargy of the senses. Any previous beauty he had seen, he continues, was unreal, his mistress's beauty being the substance or reality of beauty.

The general sense of the second stanza is plain, or *appears* to be plain. They, the two lovers, are self-sufficient, their love is their world which contains them, and in which they are contained; they have no need of further spiritual venturing forth.

> For love all love of other sights controls,
> And makes one little room, and everywhere.

The second line is ambiguous or obscure, not because of difficult words or allusions, but because, as in some modern poetry, quite simple words are used vaguely or ambiguously. The third stanza implies that the two lovers are not so much self-sufficient as complementary.

The interest of the poem does not lie in any magical use of words, in beautiful cadences, in lovely flights of fancy, or deeply penetrating imagination, but rather in the quaint subtlety and unexpectedness of the thought, and unusual turns of expression.

2. Carey's poem is in some ways the antithesis of Donne's. It is simple, popularly conventional, easy and spontaneous, expressing the love of a lad for his lass, is sentimental rather than emotional, suggesting rather the fancy of calf-love than the intensity of passion, or the depth of confirmed love. All the simple elements are there, the sweetness of Sally as compared with other lasses, the superiority of Sally to her parents, the 'abstractedness' of young lovers, the lover's pride in and concentration on the beloved object. The last line 'But not in our alley' clinches the poem emotionally. Sally is a rare object much superior to her environment.

In general, love is expressed in popular terms of 'walking out' and 'getting wed' rather than in terms of passion or possession.

The language is simple, completely lacking the incantatory element which distinguishes supremely great love poetry. It is concerned with the common objects and images of everyday life, the commonest associations being so treated as to express the purest and strongest of human sentiments. The metre is jog-trot, well adapted to the language, sentiment, and everyday associations of the poem.

3. Tennyson's poem is, in general, an invitation to a maid to descend, from the 'cold mountain tops' of learning and spiritual aloofness, to the valleys where love blooms. Let her cease to be something ethereal and apart (a sunbeam, a star). Love is lowlier, she walks among men, leaving on lonely heights things that loneliness suits, amid symbols of unfulfilled purposes. Let her not waste herself. Children call her. All the sights and sounds of home and human habitation call her.

The style is completely different from that of Donne's or Carey's poem. It is a sequence of poetic images:

The mountain height . . . symbol of chastity and female aloofness.

The Heavens . . . symbol of other-worldliness.

Sunbeam and star . . . symbols of ethereal apartness.

Happy threshold . . . symbol of human intercourse and marriage.

Death and Morning . . . symbol of cold self-denial and self-abnegation.

Dangling water-smoke . . . symbol of unfulfilled purposes.

Azure pillars of the hearth . . . symbol of home and marriage.

What is the full emotive significance of:

1. 'The splendour of the hills'?

   It conveys the idea of the frigid beauty of the denial of life, only practicable for a few dedicated spirits.

2. 'Glide a sunbeam by the blasted Pine'?
   glide suggests disembodied lightness.
   sunbeam suggests something light and ethereal.
   blasted Pine suggests isolation and frustration.
3. *Sparkling spire* suggests religion and a certain cold ethereal beauty of life.
4. *Spirted purple of the vats* suggests abundance of what delights the body rather than the soul.

8

The hard brilliant intellectual quality of some modern poetry, its affinities with the poetry of Donne, its appeal not to facile emotion, voluptuous imagery, or any of the obvious and genuine delights of the older poetry are amply illustrated in the poem by C. Day Lewis printed below:

AS ONE WHO WANDERS INTO OLD WORKINGS

As one who wanders into old workings
Dazed by the noonday, desiring coolness,
Has found retreat barred by fall of rockface;
Gropes through galleries where granite bruises
Taut palm and panic patters close at heel;
Must move forward as tide to the moon's nod,
As mouth to breast in blindness is beckoned.
Nightmare nags at his elbow and narrows
Horizon to pinpoint, hope to hand's breadth.
Slow drip the seconds, time is stalactite,
For nothing intrudes here to tell the time,
Sun marches not, nor moon with muffled step.
He wants an opening,—only to break out,
To see the dark glass cut by day's diamond,
To relax again in the lap of light.

But we seek a new world through old workings,
Whose hope lies like seed in the loins of earth,
Whose dawn draws gold from the roots of darkness
Not shy of light nor shrinking from shadow
Like Jesuits in jungle we journey
Deliberately bearing to brutish tribes
Christ's assurance, arts of agriculture
As a train that travels underground track
Feels current flashed from far-off dynamos,
Our wheels whirling with impetus elsewhere
Generated we run, are ruled by rails.
Train shall spring from tunnel to terminus,
Out on to plain shall the pioneer plunge,
Earth reveal what veins fed, what hill covered.
Lovely the leap, explosion into light.

C. DAY LEWIS

To enjoy modern poetry we must surrender ourselves to a new spirit of adventure, we must be willing to be baffled and at times depressed. Often the meaning of what we read will elude us, and even when we think we have found it we must be prepared for the discovery that, however interesting the trail we have followed, it has not led us to the particular point the poet has reached. Approached in this spirit modern poetry, and even ultra-modern poetry, will afford as keen a pleasure as the more immediately intelligible poetry of former poets, but it will be different, and to some people satisfyingly so.

The particular poem we are considering is a kind of parable. The general sense appears to be that just as a man wandering in the dark into the old workings of a mine encounters great difficulties, as he gropes his way instinctively towards the light, so modern political and social reformers, who seek change in a world where old traditions persist, must often feel their way almost intuitively through difficulties and dangers.

NOTE. One of the most interesting points to study in this poem is the series of images, some in the manner of Donne, frequently extraordinarily powerful and penetratingly imaginative, by means of which the poet develops his theme.

Panic patters . . . suggests the muffled little noises one hears when frightened in the dark.

Nightmare nags . . . the importunate obtrusion of fear.

Time is stalactite . . . hours form by the slow addition of minutes.

To see the dark glass cut by day's diamond . . . Donne-like metaphor, producing a dramatic denouement. Suddenly the darkness is cut by a thin line of light.

Lines 17 and 18. What is of value for the new social order is drawn from what is old and traditional.

Jesuits in jungle . . . Social reformers are the preachers of a new gospel.

As a train . . . far-off dynamos . . . They work blindly in the dark (underground), but the hopes of the future or tradition (far-off dynamos) inspire and drive them on.

Lovely the leap, explosion into light . . . After much underground, dark, groping working, suddenly the changes will be achieved, a dramatic revelation and attainment of the new order.

9

The following passage from one of Shakespeare's very last plays illustrates many of the features of his latest blank-verse style. It has a very high proportion of run-on lines, many lines with hypermetric syllables, and considerable variation in the position of the medial pause. Though the style is in keeping with the general level of the blank verse of the plays of this period, it lacks the supreme quality of the best passages in these plays, Prospero's speech, for example, in *The*

Tempest, Act IV, Sc. I, beginning 'These our actors', that in Act V, Sc. I, beginning 'Ye elves of brooks', Perdita's speech in *The Winter's Tale* beginning 'Now my fair'st friend', and Iachimo's in *Cymbeline*, Act II, Sc. I, beginning 'The crickets sing, and man's o'erlabour'd sense'.

Posthumus. Close by the battle, ditch'd, and wall'd with turf;
Which gave advantage to an ancient soldier,
An honest one, I warrant; who deserved
So long a breeding as his white beard came to,
In doing this for's country. Athwart the lane
He with two striplings—lads more like to run
The country base than to commit such slaughter;
With faces fit for masks, or rather fairer
Than those for preservation cased, or shame—
Made good the passage; cried to those that fled,
'Our Britain's harts die flying, not our men:
To darkness fleet souls that fly backwards. Stand;
Or we are Romans, and will give you that
Like beasts which you shun beastly, and may save
But to look back in frown: stand, stand!' These three,
Three thousand confident, in act as many,—
For three performers are the file when all
The rest do nothing,—with this word 'Stand, stand,'
Accommodated by the place, more charming
With their own nobleness, which could have turn'd
A distaff to a lance, gilded pale looks,
Part shame, part spirit renew'd; that some, turn'd coward
But by example,—O, a sin in war,
Damn'd in the first beginners!—'gan to look
The way that they did, and to grin like lions
Upon the pikes o' the hunters. Then began
A stop i' the chaser, a retire; anon
A rout, confusion thick: forthwith they fly

Chickens, the way which they stoop'd eagles; slaves,
The strides they victors made: and now our cowards,
Like fragments in hard voyages, became
The life o' the need: having found the back-door open
Of the unguarded hearts, heavens, how they wound!
Some slain before, some dying, some their friends
O'erborne i' the former wave: then chased by one
Are now each one the slaughter-man of twenty:
Those that would die or ere resist are grown
The mortal bugs o' the field.

Cymbeline

The verse of this passage, though much more natural as a vehicle for dialogue than the sweeter, more musical verse of Shakespeare's early or middle period, lacks the sweep and vigour of some of his latest blank verse, and its high imaginative quality. It is more prosaic in style, but for one important reservation, its compressed metaphors, some of which are commented upon below. It is, however, very workmanlike, and gives a vivid picture of the scene described.

NOTE.

Like beasts which you shun beastly—will slaughter you like the beasts (harts), which you imitate by running.

turn'd a distaff to a lance—made even a woman fight.

Then began a stop i' the chaser—the pursuers were halted.

they fly chickens . . . stoop'd eagles—the bold Romans who before had pounced on their foe like eagles, now became runaways.

slaves, the strides they victors made—The Romans went back slaves (conquered men) the very way they had come as victors.

Like fragments in hard voyages, became the life o' the need—Like bits of food in hard voyages, they became just what was needed for life and safety.

Having found the back-door open of the unguarded hearts—they stabbed their enemy to the heart *from behind*.

Mortal bugs o' the field—death-dealing terrors of the battle-field.

Any obscurity there is in the passages above is due to the fact that the figurative language which abounds in them is compressed and has to be expanded to make the sense clear.

Exercises on Chapter VII

I. Read through the following speech carefully, then answer the questions printed below:

K. Richard. No matter where; of comfort no man speak:
Let's talk of graves, of worms and epitaphs;
Make dust our paper and with rainy eyes
Write sorrow on the bosom of the earth.
Let's choose executors and talk of wills:
And yet not so, for what can we bequeath
Save our deposed bodies to the ground?
Our lands, our lives and all are Bolingbroke's,
And nothing can we call our own but death,
And that small model of the barren earth
Which serves as paste and cover to our bones.
For God's sake, let us sit upon the ground
And tell sad stories of the death of kings:
How some have been deposed; some slain in war;
Some haunted by the ghosts they have deposed;
Some poisoned by their wives; some sleeping killed;
All murder'd: for within the hollow crown
That rounds the mortal temples of a king
Keeps Death his court, and there the antic sits,
Scoffing his state and grinning at his pomp,
Allowing him a breath, a little scene,
To monarchize, be fear'd and kill with looks,
Infusing him with self and vain conceit,
As if this flesh which walls about our life
Were brass impregnable, and humour'd thus
Comes at the last and with a little pin
Bores through his castle wall, and farewell king!

Cover your heads and mock not flesh and blood
With solemn reverence: throw away respect,
Tradition, form and ceremonious duty,
For you have but mistook me all this while:
I live with bread like you, feel want,
Taste grief, need friends: subjected thus,
How can you say to me, I am a king?

The Tragedy of King Richard II

QUESTIONS

1. What is the prevailing mood in this speech?
2. What is the meaning of the phrase 'Make dust our paper?
3. Many people resemble the speaker in temperament. Would they normally express themselves in the same way? If not, wherein does his mode of speech differ?
4. What is the meaning of 'that small model of the barren earth Which serves as paste and cover to our bones'?
5. Why 'antic'?
6. What is the full emotive force of the word *breath*, as used here?
7. What is the force of the phrase 'little pin', as used here?
8. What qualities of kingship are suggested in the last line?
9. What is the meaning of the word *macabre*? What evidence of the *macabre* do you find in this passage?

II. Read carefully through the following poem, and then answer the questions printed below:

Three years she grew in sun and shower;
Then Nature said, 'A lovelier flower
  On earth was never sown:
This child I to myself will take;
She shall be mine, and I will make
  A lady of my own.

'Myself will to my darling be
Both law and impulse: and with me
  The girl, in rock and plain,
In earth and heaven, in glade and bower,
Shall feel an overseeing power
  To kindle or restrain.

'She shall be sportive as the fawn
That wild with glee across the lawn
  Or up the mountain springs;

And hers shall be the breathing balm,
And hers the silence and the calm
  Of mute insensate things.

'The floating clouds their state shall lend
To her; for her the willow bend;
  Nor shall she fail to see
E'en in the motions of the storm
Grace that shall mould the maiden's form
  By silent sympathy.

'The stars of midnight shall be dear
To her; and she shall lean her ear
  In many a secret place
Where rivulets dance their wayward round,
And beauty born of murmuring sound
  Shall pass into her face.

'And vital feelings of delight
Shall rear her form to stately height,
  Her virgin bosom swell;
Such thoughts to Lucy I will give
While she and I together live
  Here in this happy dell.'

Thus Nature spake—The work was done—
How soon my Lucy's race was run!
  She died, and left to me
This heath, this calm and quiet scene;
The memory of what has been,
  And never more will be.

WILLIAM WORDSWORTH

QUESTIONS

1. What is the idea running through this poem?
2. Explain the meaning of the phrase, 'Both law and impulse'?
3. Which do you consider the finest stanza? Justify fully your choice.
4. In what lines does the sound most subtly echo the sense?
5. What exactly does the poet mean here by 'To kindle or restrain'?
6. What physical characteristics in the girl are suggested by lines 19–20 and 22–4?

7. If this is, in your opinion, a good poem, what definition of 'good poetry' do you think it best illustrates? If not a 'good poem' what are the qualities of a good poem it most conspicuously lacks?

8. Do you think the metre of this poem well adapted to the subject? Give full reasons for your answer.

III. Read carefully the following three curses, taken from Shakespeare's plays, and then answer the questions printed below:

1. *Timon.* Let me look back on thee. O thou wall,
That girdlest in those wolves, dive in the earth,
And fence not Athens! . . .
Obedience fail in children! Slaves and fools,
Pluck the grave wrinkled senate from the bench,
And minister in their steads! . . .
Bankrupts, hold fast;
Rather than render back, out with your knives,
And cut your trusters' throats! Bound servants, steal!
Large-handed robbers your grave masters are
And pill by law. . . .
Son of sixteen,
Pluck the lined crutch from thy old limping sire,
With it beat out his brains! Piety and fear,
Religion to the gods, peace, justice, truth,
Domestic awe, night-rest and neighbourhood,
Instruction, manners, mysteries and trades,
Degrees, observances, customs and laws,
Decline to your confounding contraries,
And let confusion live! Plagues incident to men,
Your potent and infectious fevers heap
On Athens, ripe for stroke! Thou cold sciatica,
Cripple our senators, that their limbs may halt
As lamely as their manners! Lust and liberty
Creep in the minds and marrows of our youth,
That 'gainst the stream of virtue they may strive,
And drown themselves in riot! Itches, blains,
Sow all the Athenian bosoms, and their crop
Be general leprosy! Breath infect breath,
That their society, as their friendship, may
Be merely poison! Nothing I'll bear from thee
But nakedness, thou detestable town!

Take thou that too, with multiplying bans!
Timon will to the woods, where he shall find
The unkindest beast more kinder than mankind.
The gods confound—hear me, you good gods all!
The Athenians both within and out that wall!
And grant, as Timon grows, his hate may grow
To the whole race of mankind, high and low!
Amen. *Timon of Athens*

2. *Coriolanus.* You common cry of curs! whose breath I hate
As reek o' the rotten fens, whose loves I prise
As the dead carcasses of unburied men
That do corrupt my air, I banish you;
And here remain with your uncertainty!
Let every feeble rumour shake your hearts!
Your enemies, with nodding of their plumes,
Fan you into despair! Have the power still
To banish your defenders; till at length
Your ignorance, which finds not till it feels,
Making not reservation of yourselves,
Still your own foes, deliver you as most
Abated captives to some nation
That won you without blows! Despising,
For you, the city, thus I turn my back:
There is a world elsewhere. *Coriolanus*

3. *Lear.* Hear, nature, hear; dear goddess, hear!
Suspend thy purpose, if thou didst intend
To make this creature fruitful:
Into her womb convey sterility:
Dry up in her the organs of increase,
And from her derogate body never spring
A babe to honour her! If she must teem,
Create her child of spleen, that it may live
And be a thwart disnatured torment to her.
Let it stamp wrinkles in her brow of youth;
With cadent tears fret channels in her cheeks;
Turn all her mother's pains and benefits
To laughter and contempt; that she may feel
How sharper than a serpent's tooth it is
To have a thankless child! *King Lear*

QUESTIONS

1. Who, or what, is the object of the curse in each of these three poems respectively?

2. Which of the curses is the most terrible, and shows the deepest pessimism?

3. Which reveals a man most terribly wrenched from natural feeling?

4. Which shows rather outraged pride than a violent upheaval in the soul?

5. What common inspiration or generating motive had they?

6. Compare and contrast the passages with regard to their blank verse style.

7. What is the most dreadful single thing Lear says?

8. Lear says *one* thing four times. Is this mere repetition?

9. There is a curious division in the passage from *Timon of Athens*? In what way are the two parts of the passage, thus divided, different?

IV. Read carefully the poem printed below, and then answer the questions.

ANIMULA

'Issues from the hand of God, the simple soul'
To a flat world of changing lights and noise,
To light, dark, dry or damp, chilly or warm;
Moving between the legs of tables and of chairs,
Rising or falling, grasping at kisses and toys,
Advancing boldly, sudden to take alarm,
Retreating to the corner of arm and knee,
Eager to be reassured, taking pleasure
In the fragrant brilliance of the Christmas tree,
Pleasure in the wind, the sunlight and the sea;
Studies the sunlit pattern on the floor
And running stags around a silver tray;
Confounds the actual and the fanciful,
Content with playing-cards and kings and queens,
What the fairies do and what the servants say.
The heavy burden of the growing soul
Perplexes and offends more, day by day;
Week by week, offends and perplexes more
With the imperatives of 'is and seems'

And may and may not, desire and control.
The pain of living and the drug of dreams
Curl up the small soul in the window seat
Behind the *Encyclopaedia Britannica*.
Issues from the hand of time the simple soul
Irresolute and selfish, misshapen, lame,
Unable to fare forward or retreat,
Fearing the warm reality, the offered good,
Denying the importunity of the blood,
Shadow of its own shadows, spectre in its own gloom,
Leaving disordered papers in a dusty room;
Living first in the silence after the viaticum.
Pray for Guiterriez, avid of speed and power,
For Boudin, blown to pieces,
For this one who made a great fortune,
And that one who went his own way.
Pray for Floret, by the boarhound slain between the yew trees,
Pray for us now and at the hour of our birth.

THOMAS STEARNS ELIOT

QUESTIONS

1. Describe the metre of the poem.

2. How is the poem constructed? Describe precisely its logical arrangement.

3. What definition of poetry would make the best starting-point for an appreciation of this poem?

4. What merits of some good poetry does this poem lack?

5. What characteristics of modern poetry does it exhibit?

6. What evidence does this poem afford that the writer has really studied children from babyhood?

7. Explain the full significance of the word 'perplexes' as used in this poem. A mere dictionary definition will not do.

8. Explain the full significance of the *imperatives of 'is and seems'*.

9. Explain fully the meaning of the following lines:

> The pain of living and the drug of dreams
> Curl up the small soul in the window seat.

10. What exactly is meant by:

> Shadow of its own shadows, spectre in its own gloom?

11. Explain fully the meaning of the word 'importunity' and its significance in the poem.

12. What line suggests the influence of modern (Freudian) psychology?

13. What feelings or emotions does the poem arouse?

V. Read carefully the poem printed below, and then answer the questions:

Two voices are there, one is of the Sea,
    One of the mountains, each a mighty voice:
    In both from age to age thou didst rejoice,
They were thy chosen music, Liberty!

There came a tyrant, and with holy glee
    Thou fought'st against him,—but hast vainly striven:
    Thou from thy Alpine holds at length art driven,
Where not a torrent murmurs heard by thee.

Of one deep bliss thine ear hath been bereft;
Then cleave, O cleave to that which still is left;
    For high-soul'd Maid, what sorrow would it be

    That Mountain floods should thunder as before,
    And Ocean bellow from his rocky shore,
And neither awful Voice be heard by Thee!

WILLIAM WORDSWORTH

QUESTIONS

1. State briefly the theme of the poem.
2. Examine the sequence of thoughts and images in the poem.
3. What is the form of the poem? Is the rhyming structure a usual one for this kind of poem?
4. Scan lines 1 and 2.
5. Show how the sound echoes the sense in this poem.
6. What is there particularly happy in the repetition of the word 'cleave'?
7. What is there particularly happy in the use of the word 'music'?
8. What is the unity of the poem?

VI. Read carefully the following poem, and then answer the questions printed below:

It is not true that eyes
Save in the trembling eyelids' fall and rise

No meaning have. Did Eve
Hide in dull orbs the Snake's guile, and deceive
Adam with innocent stare?
When David saw how Bathsheba was fair
Burnt in his eyes no fire?
Marked not the men-at-arms his flushed desire
Sudden and swift upbrim,
That not the falling eyelids' cloud could dim?
And when Prince Absalon
Hung by those fatal locks, and help was none,
Under the nerveless lid
How could his father's agony be hid?
He heard the whisper, heard
The hushing, the renewed whisper, the one word:
And then was such gaze
As between madness and first wild grief sways,
Till 'Absalon!' and no sound
But 'Absalon, my son, my son!' crept round.
It is not true that eyes
No meaning have but in the lids' fall and rise.
I have seen terror leap
Up from the spirit's unfathomable deep,
Through unfixed eyeballs stare,
Then shuddering sink back and lie snake-like there.
I have seen honour look
Swift under candid brows, when all else shook,
Pouring in warm light through
Eyes that from inward vision their seeing drew.
And I know the fluttering look
That first love flashes like a bird o'er a brook . . .
No lid so quick as to give
Speed to the glances that with lightning live.
And I know how the eyes
Nameless, look on me out of clear dawn skies
And eve's unshadowy light—
Clear lidless eyes of pure immortal sight,
Sweeping the million dew'd
Hill pastures and reluming the green-caved wood.

JOHN FREEMAN

QUESTIONS

1. Explain briefly the theme of the poem.
2. How is the theme developed?
3. What variations are there on the phrase, 'It is not true'?
4. What differing emotive values have the following phrases?
   (*a*) trembling eyelids' fall and rise.
   (*b*) sudden and swift upbrim.
   (*c*) nerveless lid.
   (*d*) swift under candid brows.
   (*e*) fluttering look.
5. Why is the word 'orbs' used for eyes in line 4?
6. Why is the word 'cloud' used in line 10?
7. What is there noteworthy about line 16?
8. What does line 26 suggest by its rhythm and phrasing?
9. What is there noteworthy about line 32?
10. What are the 'clear lidless eyes'? Why are they so called?

VII. Read carefully the following poem, and then answer the questions printed below:

TO EVENING

If aught of oaten stop or pastoral song
May hope, O pensive Eve, to soothe thine ear,
  Like thy own brawling springs,
  Thy springs, and dying gales;

O Nymph reserved,—while now the bright-hair'd sun
Sits in yon western tent, whose cloudy skirts
  With brede ethereal wove
  O'erhang his wavy bed;

Now air is hush'd, save where the weak-ey'd bat
With short shrill shriek flits by on leathern wing,
  Or where the beetle winds
  His small but sullen horn,

As oft he rises 'midst the twilight path,
Against the pilgrim borne in heedless hum,—
  Now teach me, maid composed,
  To breathe some soften'd strain,

Whose numbers, stealing through thy dark'ning vale,
May not unseemly with its stillness suit;
  As musing slow I hail
  Thy genial loved return.

For when thy folding-star arising shows
His paly circlet, at his warning lamp
  The fragrant Hours, and Elves
  Who slept in buds the day,

And many a Nymph who wreathes her brows with sedge
And sheds the freshening dew, and lovelier still
  The pensive Pleasures sweet,
  Prepare thy shadowy car.

Then let me rove some wild and heathy scene;
Or find some ruin midst its dreary dells,
  Whose walls more awful nod
  By thy religious gleams.

Or if chill blustering winds or driving rain
Prevent my willing feet, be mine the hut
  That from the mountain's side,
  Views wilds or swelling floods,

And hamlets brown, and dim-discover'd spires;
And hears their simple bell; and marks o'er all
  Thy dewy fingers draw
  The gradual dusky veil.

While Spring shall pour his showers, as oft he wont,
And bathe thy breathing tresses, meekest Eve!
  While Summer loves to sport
  Beneath thy lingering light;

While sallow Autumn fills thy lap with leaves;
Or Winter, yelling through the troublous air,
  Affrights thy shrinking train
  And rudely rends thy robes;

So long regardless of thy quiet rule,
Shall Fancy, Friendship, Science, smiling Peace,
  Thy gentlest influence own,
  And love thy favourite name!

WILLIAM COLLINS

QUESTIONS

1. What is the theme of the poem?

2. In what way does this eighteenth-century poem look forward to Romanticism, and to the poetry of Wordsworth in particular?

3. In what way is it of the eighteenth century?

4. What is the metre of the poem?

5. What is there metrically peculiar about the third stanza?

6. What is the most appealing picture of evening in the poem?

7. Pick out three stanzas which might form subjects of three quite different kinds of picture. Describe the pictures as you would imagine the artists might paint them.

8. What evidence of Celtic influence can be found in the poem?

9. In what stanzas is the influence of the eighteenth century most apparent? Support your answer fully.

10. Quote examples of the echoing of the sense by the sound. Show how these effects are brought about.

11. What two lines most suggest the uncanny quiet of evening? How is this achieved?

12. Discuss the imagery of the poem.

VIII. Read carefully the two following poems, and then answer the questions printed below:

PRELUDES III AND IV

III.

You tossed a blanket from the bed,
You lay upon your back and waited;
You dozed, and watched the night revealing
The thousand sordid images
Of which your soul was constituted;
They flickered against the ceiling.
And when all the world came back
And the light crept up between the shutters,
And you heard the sparrows in the gutters,
You had such a vision of the street
As the street hardly understands;
Sitting along the bed's edge, where
You curled the papers from your hair,
Or clasped the yellow soles of feet
In the palms of both soiled hands.

IV. His soul stretched tight across the skies
That fade behind a city block,
Or trampled by insistent feet
At four and five and six o'clock;
And short square fingers stuffing pipes,
And evening newspapers, and eyes
Assured of certain certainties,
The conscience of a blackened street
Impatient to assume the world.
I am moved by fancies that are curled
Around these images, and cling:
The notion of some infinitely gentle
Infinitely suffering thing.
Wipe your hand across your mouth, and laugh;
The worlds revolve like ancient women
Gathering fuel in vacant lots.

THOMAS STEARNS ELIOT

QUESTIONS

(III)

1. What is the unity of this poem?

2. How is the particular mood, which is the unity of the poem, generated?

3. Trace the thought of the poem.

4. What is the significance for this poem of the line, 'You curled the papers from your hair'?

5. What different types of image are evoked by the phrase 'yellow soles of feet'?

(IV)

1. What is the unifying mood in this poem?

2. Show how the theme is developed.

3. Explain the significance for the poem of the phrases 'four and five and six o'clock', 'short square fingers', 'evening newspapers', 'certain certainties'.

4. Later on in the poem there is a feeling of revulsion from the original mood of the poem. What is the mood of this feeling of revulsion?

5. This is followed by another abrupt change of mood. What is this mood?

6. What have the 'ancient women' got to do with the subject?

IX. Read carefully through the following poem, and answer the questions printed below:

IN MEMORIAM F.A.S.

Yet, O stricken heart, remember, O remember
 How of human days he lived the better part.
April came to bloom and never chill December
 Breathed its killing chills upon the head or heart.

Doomed to know not Winter, only Spring, a being
 Trod the flowery April blithely for a while,
Took his fill of music, joy of thought and seeing,
 Came and stayed and went, nor ever ceased to smile.

Came and stayed and went, and now when all is finished,
 You alone have crossed the melancholy stream,
Yours the pang, but his, O his, the undiminished
 Undecaying gladness, undeparted dream.

All that life contains of torture, toil and treason,
 Shame, dishonour, death, to him were but a name.
Here, a boy, he dwelt through all the singing season
 And ere the day of sorrow departed as he came.

ROBERT LOUIS STEVENSON

QUESTIONS

1. What is the unity of idea in this poem?
2. Trace the sequence of thought.
3. Discuss the imagery of the poem.
4. Explain fully the form and metrical structure of the poem.
5. What words and phrases suggest most emotively the time of youth?
6. What four lines would appeal most, do you think, to anyone who had lost a child? Why?
7. Compare and contrast this poem with another on the same or a similar theme.
8. Using this poem as the source of material for a definition of poetry, compose a definition.

X. Read carefully through the following three poems, and then answer the questions printed below:

1. Now sleeps the crimson petal, now the white;
Nor waves the cypress in the palace walk;
Nor winks the gold fin in the porphyry font:
The fire-fly wakens: waken thou with me.

Now droops the milkwhite peacock like a ghost,
And like a ghost she glimmers on to me.

Now lies the Earth all Danaë to the stars,
And all thy heart lies open unto me.

Now slides the silent meteor on, and leaves
A shining furrow, as thy thoughts in me.

Now folds the lily all her sweetness up,
And slips into the bosom of the lake:
So fold thyself, my dearest, thou, and slip
Into my bosom and be lost in me.

LORD TENNYSON

2. The splendour falls on castle walls
And snowy summits old in story:
The long light shakes across the lakes,
And the wild cataract leaps in glory.
Blow, bugle; blow, set the wild echoes flying,
Blow, bugle, answer, echoes, dying, dying, dying.

O hark, O hear! how thin and clear,
And thinner, clearer, farther going!
O sweet and far from cliff and scar
The horns of Elfland faintly blowing!
Blow, let us hear the purple glens replying:
Blow, bugle, answer, echoes, dying, dying, dying.

O love, they die in yon rich sky,
They faint on hill or field or river:
Our echoes roll from soul to soul,
And grow for ever and for ever.
Blow, bugle, blow, set the wild echoes flying,
And answer, echoes, answer dying, dying, dying.

LORD TENNYSON

3. Tears, idle tears, I know not what they mean,
Tears from the depth of some divine despair
Rise in the heart, and gather to the eyes,
In looking on the happy Autumn-fields,
And thinking of the days that are no more.

Fresh as the first beam glittering on a sail,
That brings our friends up from the underworld,
Sad as the last which reddens over one
That sinks with all we love below the verge;
So sad, so fresh, the days that are no more.

Ah, sad and strange as in dark summer dawns
The earliest pipe of half-awaken'd birds
To dying ears, when unto dying eyes
The casement slowly grows a glimmering square;
So sad, so strange, the days that are no more.

Dear as remember'd kisses after death,
And sweet as those by hopeless fancy feign'd
On lips that are for others; deep as love,
Deep as first love, and wild with all regret;
O Death in Life, the days that are no more.

LORD TENNYSON

QUESTIONS

1. 'Here are three of the greatest lyrics in the language', said the late Mr. Humbert Wolfe. Do you agree with this high praise? Support your answer fully.

2. Examine the thought of the first poem, and show how it is developed. Write notes on the metre.

3. Discuss the appropriateness of the image by which the conclusion is prepared for.

4. Why is the peacock described as *milkwhite*?

5. Explain the allusion in the seventh line.

6. Why a *shining* furrow?

7. What is the precise meaning of the last two lines?

8. What line or lines do you most admire? Justify your choice.

9. What is the poem *The Splendour Falls* all about?

10. What significance for the poem as a whole have the two lines,

> Our echoes roll from soul to soul,
> And grow for ever and for ever?

11. What line or lines do you most admire in the poem?

12. Trace the thought and images in the third poem.

13. What is the metre of the poem?

14. What is the point of lines 11 to 14?

15. Do any lines strike you as particularly beautiful or emotive? Support your answer fully.

16. What is the precise meaning of 'hopeless fancy'?

XI. Read carefully through the following poem, and then answer the questions printed below:

When I have fears that I may cease to be
  Before my pen has glean'd my teeming brain,
Before high-piled books, in charactry
  Hold like rich garners the full-ripen'd grain;

When I behold, upon the night's starr'd face,
  Huge cloudy symbols of a high romance,
And think that I may never live to trace
  Their shadows, with the magic hand of chance;

And when I feel, fair creature of an hour!
  That I shall never look upon thee more,
Never have relish in the fairy power
  Of unreflecting love—then on the shore

Of the wide world I stand alone, and think
Till love and fame to nothingness do sink.

JOHN KEATS

QUESTIONS

1. State briefly the theme of the poem.

2. Examine the sequence of images, and show how the thought of the poem is developed by them.

3. How is the unity of the poem achieved?

4. What image most interests or pleases you?

5. What four lines are richest in imagery? Analyse the imagery.

6. From the material before you in this poem compose a definition of poetry.

7. Analyse the metrical structure of this poem, and then state to what general type of poem it belongs, and to what particular species of that type.

XII. Read carefully through the following poem, and then answer the questions printed below:

1. O wild West Wind, thou breath of Autumn's being,
   Thou, from whose unseen presence the leaves dead
Are driven, like ghosts from an enchanter fleeing,

Yellow, and black, and pale, and hectic red,
   Pestilence-stricken multitudes: O thou
Who chariotest to their dark wintry bed

The winged seeds, where they lie cold and low,
   Each like a corpse within its grave, until
Thine azure sister of the Spring shall blow

Her clarion o'er the dreaming earth, and fill
   (Driving sweet buds like flocks to feed in air)
With living hues and odours plain and hill:

Wild Spirit, which art moving everywhere;
Destroyer and Preserver; hear, oh, hear!

2. Thou on whose stream, mid the steep sky's commotion,
   Loose clouds like earth's decaying leaves are shed,
Shook from the tangled boughs of Heaven and Ocean,

Angels of rain and lightning: there are spread
   On the blue surface of thine airy surge,
Like the bright hair uplifted from the head

Of some fierce Maenad, even from the dim verge
   Of the horizon to the zenith's height,
The locks of the approaching storm. Thou dirge

Of the dying year, to which this closing night
   Will be the dome of a vast sepulchre,
Vaulted with all thy congregated might

Of vapours, from whose solid atmosphere
Black rain, and fire, and hail, will burst: oh hear!

3. Thou who didst waken from his summer dreams
   The blue Mediterranean, where he lay,
Lull'd by the coil of his crystalline streams,

Beside a pumice isle in Baiae's bay,
  And saw in sleep old palaces and towers
Quivering within the wave's intenser day,

All overgrown with azure moss and flowers
  So sweet, the sense faints picturing them! Thou
For whose path the Atlantic's level powers

Cleave themselves into chasms, while far below
  The sea-blooms and the oozy woods which wear
The sapless foliage of the ocean, know

Thy voice, and suddenly grow grey with fear,
And tremble and despoil themselves: oh, hear!

4. If I were a dead leaf thou mightest bear;
  If I were a swift cloud to fly with thee;
A wave to pant beneath thy power, and share

The impulse of thy strength, only less free
  Than thou, O uncontrollable! If even
I were as in my boyhood, and could be

The comrade of thy wanderings over Heaven,
  As then, when to outstrip thy skyey speed
Scarce seemed a vision, I would ne'er have striven

As thus with thee in prayer in my sore need.
  Oh, lift me as a wave, a leaf, a cloud!
I fall upon the thorns of life! I bleed!

A heavy weight of hours has chained and bowed
One too like thee: tameless, and swift, and proud.

5. Make me thy lyre, even as the forest is:
  What if my leaves are falling like its own!
The tumult of thy mighty harmonies

Will take from both a deep, autumnal tone,
  Sweet though in sadness. Be thou, Spirit fierce,
My spirit! Be thou me, impetuous one!

Drive my dead thoughts over the universe
  Like withered leaves to quicken a new birth!
And, by the incantation of this verse,

Scatter, as from an unextinguished hearth
  Ashes and sparks, my words among mankind!
Be through my lips to unawakened earth

The trumpet of a prophecy! O Wind,
If Winter comes, can Spring be far behind?

P. B. SHELLEY

QUESTIONS

1. Explain in about twenty-five words what is the theme of the poem.

2. What is the metre of the poem?

3. What are the most striking characteristics of the poem?

4. What do you consider the finest examples of visual imagery in the poem?

5. What do you consider the finest examples of aural imagery?

6. For what reasons cannot the five sections of the poem be regarded as sonnets?

7. Which section comes nearest to being a sonnet? In what respect is it like a sonnet? In what is it not?

8. Show how occasionally in this poem words bearing a very heavy rhythmic stress bear also an emotive stress.

9. What four colours stand out in your mind after reading this poem? What abstract ideas do they symbolize?

XIII. Read carefully the following poem, and then answer the questions that follow it:

Break, break, break,
  On thy cold grey stones, O Sea!
And I would that my tongue could utter
  The thoughts that arise in me.

O well for the fisherman's boy,
  That he shouts with his sister at play!
O well for the sailor lad,
  That he sings in his boat on the bay!

And the stately ships go on
  To their haven under the hill;
But O for the touch of a vanished hand;
  And the sound of a voice that is still!

Break, break, break,
  At the foot of thy crags, O Sea!
But the tender grace of a day that is dead
  Will never come back to me.

LORD TENNYSON

QUESTIONS

(*a*) State briefly the theme of the poem.

(*b*) Examine the sequence of images, thoughts, &c., through the poem, showing their relationship and connexion.

DATE DUE

JUN 19 '80			
JUN 30 '83			

Glassey

The groundwork of criticism

Due Date	1st Ren.	2nd Ren.

Glassey

The groundwork of criticism